David Beckham

Fantastic Lessons From an English Football Legend

(The History of the World's Famous Football Legend)

Noe Spain

Published By **Cathy Nedrow**

Noe Spain

All Rights Reserved

David Beckham: Fantastic Lessons From an English Football Legend (The History of the World's Famous Football Legend)

ISBN 978-1-7775276-9-3

No part of this guidebook shall be reproduced in any form without permission in writing from the publisher except in the case of brief quotations embodied in critical articles or reviews.

Legal & Disclaimer

The information contained in this book is not designed to replace or take the place of any form of medicine or professional medical advice. The information in this book has been provided for educational & entertainment purposes only.

The information contained in this book has been compiled from sources deemed reliable, and it is accurate to the best of the Author's knowledge; however, the Author cannot guarantee its accuracy and validity and cannot be held liable for any errors or omissions. Changes are periodically made to this book. You must consult your doctor or get professional medical advice before using any of the suggested remedies, techniques, or information in this book.

Upon using the information contained in this book, you agree to hold harmless the Author from and against any damages, costs, and expenses, including any legal fees potentially resulting from the application of any of the information provided by this guide. This disclaimer applies to any damages or injury caused by the use and application, whether directly or indirectly, of any advice or information presented, whether for breach of contract, tort, negligence, personal injury, criminal intent, or under any other cause of action.

You agree to accept all risks of using the information presented inside this book. You need to consult a professional medical practitioner in order to ensure you are both able and healthy enough to participate in this program.

Table Of Contents

Chapter 1: Groomed For Football 1

Chapter 2: Posh And Becks 17

Chapter 3: The Gods Of Football Both Scowled And Smiled 23

Chapter 4: The Journey From Manchester To Madrid 32

Chapter 5: From Madrid To L.A. 48

Chapter 6: The Beckham Galaxy Traveling With David 54

Chapter 7: Here And Back 59

Chapter 8: Still Kickin And Even After The Field 67

Chapter 9: The Little Red Devil 72

Chapter 10: Together With Bobby Charlton 85

Chapter 11: Kevin Keegan 104

Chapter 12: World Cup 1998 132

Chapter 13: A Golden Year 155

Chapter 14: Mclaren Confronts Ellery .. 165

Chapter 15: Beckham Kisses Son Brooklyn
.... 179

Chapter 1: Groomed For Football

The 2nd of May in 1975, David Joseph Robert Beckham was born to David Edward Allan and Sandra Georgina Beckham in Whipps Cross University Hospital, Leytonstone, and London, England. David was the second and the only child in the trio of children. As his eyes began to open up towards the world, benefits of the lifestyle of a famous person did not exist for the baby David to see.

The father of David, known to his family and friends as Ted is a modest kitchen fitting and his mother was a hairdresser. David's maternal grandfather on his family was Jewish. Although David himself admits to later on that he may have been more involved with Judaism in comparison to other religions, and would eventually believe that he was "half Jewish", he was a regular attender at church every Sunday alongside his parents as well as siblings

Lynne Georgina as well as Joanne Louise. Like many blue collared inhabitants in Leytonstone the Beckhams were able to do all they could to be able to through the day and offer education to their three kids.

Sports fans

However, the only fact that can be stated concerning the Beckham couple is they were huge fans of Manchester United and frequently traveled from Leytonstone in the London neighborhood of Leytonstone up to Trafford in order to go to the matches of Manchester United. They would cheer, shout and yell for their favourite team, and would scream for hours if informed that Manchester United was not the greatest football team around.

The sole son of Ted eventually took on his parents' love for the team and to the game, and their passion and commitment to everyday life. The Beckhams depended on the money Ted could offer by his shaky earnings. After observing young David's enthusiasm for soccer, Ted made sure his son had the gear that he needed, as the majority of his free time was spent in Ridgeway Park.

Youthful dreams

David initially attended Chase Lane primary school when he was a youngster and then was transferred into Chingford Foundation School. If his teachers ever asked him what he would like to do when he was older with, he could give an easy reply: play professional football. His teachers regarded this as an unrealistic child's dream and then demanded David what would be the ideal career he wanted to pursue and hoping to get answers like becoming a doctor or pilot. But David did not back down. David wanted to become an elite footballer only.

"At school whenever the teachers asked, 'What do you want to do when you're older?' I'd say, 'I want to be a footballer.'

And they'd say, 'No, what do you really want to do, for a job?' But that was the only thing I ever wanted to do." He said this in an interview in 2007.

The path to the realization of this goal began by playing with the Ridgway Rovers from the Enfield District League. The team was led by Stuart Underwood, Steve Kirby and Ted himself. When he was just eighteen, David scored for the Rovers more than a hundred goals over the course of three seasons. Evidently, this proved that David was a special player and had an ability that was worthy of nurturing.

David was eleven years old. David was eleven years old, Ted enrolled him at one of Bobby Charlton's Football Schools in Manchester, in which David then took part in a talent show known as Bobby Charlton Soccer Skills. David won the opportunity to attend an intense two-week session of training with FC Barcelona.

It seemed like it could be an enjoyable ride. But the first bump in the road was when he attempted to secure an opportunity with the Junior English League. David was turned down for being too small considering his age. It's unclear what David reacts to this however the one thing that is sure was that it didn't hinder him from having an athletic career in his early years.

The next time he was involved in football was playing as the character of Manchester United when they went heads-to-head in a match against West Ham in 1986. Then, David tried his luck playing with Leyton Orient first then again at Spurs' School of Excellence. The first team David Beckham played for was Tottenham Hotspurs. After that Beckham was a member of the team's youth squad of Brimsdown Rovers. He showed the potential to be selected as the 1990's Under 15 Player of the Year.

Beckham was then a student at Bradenton Preparatory Academy. He did not attend school for very lengthy as the team that he had a love for since the age of a child had hoped to have them under their wing. At the age of fourteen, David was fourteen years old in 1989 and was still playing for Brimsdown Rovers, he joined the Brimsdown Rovers club, he filled out student forms with Manchester United. On July 8, 1991, he had been awarded his Youth Training Scheme Contract.

Fergie's Fledglings

David joined a skilled group of club youngsters, referred to in the nickname "Fergie's Fledglings" - with Fergie being Manchester United manager Sir Alex Ferguson. The youngsters included were future international footballers like Phil as well as Gary Neville, Nick Butt, Paul Scholes and Ryan Giggs. They were among the youngsters who took home the FA Youth Cup in May in 1992. It is David himself, who was the one to score the second match with Crystal Palace in the event's finals.

That similar year, David Beckham made his first appearance for Manchester United when they went against Brighton as well as Hove Abion in a League Cup. David Beckham could have been a an extra in that game and it was until a few months later that David Beckham signed his debut professional deal at Manchester United. Following the calendar year David along with his teammates made it to the semifinals of the Youth Cup though they were ultimately defeated to Leeds United. in 1994, David received a third award as Manchester United's reserve team was crowned the League.

To get that necessary first team knowledge, David went to Preston North End to be on loan to Manchester United for the 1994-1995 season. When he returned to the team he was playing for on the 2nd of April 1995, he played his first appearance in the Premier League for them against the Leeds. The match ended in an uncontested draw.

David's debut for his time with the England National Football Team came later in the year, on the 1st of September in 1996. It was played against Moldova to play the World Cup Qualifying Match. It was clear that the 17-year young David Beckham was looking at an extremely promising career path in the sport he'd often imagined as a kid. David Beckham didn't let this accomplishment get in his thoughts however. He pushed himself to the limit and further to develop his techniques. He was a great coach. Alex Ferguson was quoted as declaring that David was disciplined in his training that he was able to reach a level precision that most players don't bother about.

It wasn't solely his desire to succeed which drove David striving for more in spite of pain and challenges that came from being a young man. Parents constantly stayed by his side and to encourage him in the sense that hardship can be the steward of accomplishment in that the victory of determination and determination to overcome challenges is at the heart of all. This is why it was that he took his strength. Also, Ted and Sandra didn't simply help David through words. If they were able to they were constant friends and gave him whatever David could have wanted. "They followed me everywhere, paid for me to go everywhere, paid for me to have new boots and new footballs and stuff like that," the man stated in an interview a few several years after the fact.

2. The beginning of something truly extraordinary

There was no fact the fact that Manchester United Manager Sir Alex Ferguson was full of trust in the younger players that he gathered in his squad. He was a shrewd observer of talent and was perhaps greater than other managers had seen in his "Fergie's Fledgelings". Thus, at the close of 1994-1995, when the experienced player

Mark Huges, Paul Ince and Andrei Kanchelskis hung their Manchester United uniforms Fergie chose to substitute them by players from his young team instead of buying stars from different clubs.

The move was met with a great deal of criticism from both fans as well as the press. The criticism grew after Manchester United began the season by a 3-1 loss to Aston Villa. The sole goal scored by Manchester United in the match was scored by David. Fergie wasn't deterred and was determined to stick to his game plan. He knew that his "fledglings' could do it, and therefore he refused to allow himself to be swayed by tension. He continued to fight. As Manchester United won their next following five games, and Fergie's Fledglings showed their value The critics were quieted.

In the beginning, it appeared like Beckham was not going to win his first championship medal this season, as Manchester United was still ten points back from Newcastle

United. But, in mid-March, David and his team teammates beat Tynesiders and continued to be on top of the table until season's final.

This was the year the season that David Beckham quickly established himself as the right-sided midfielder for the team. He veered from what the rest of the team were expecting of his performance in the field (a right winger similar to the great Andrei Kanchelskis) and helped Manchester United bag FA Cup double as well as the Premier League title that season. He scored the game-winning goal in the semi-final game against Chelsea and provided his teammate Eric Cantona the corner needed to get a goal scored during the FA Cup Final.

The wrong Shoes

On the 17th of August, 1996 on the first day of the 1996-97 Premier League, David Beckham established his name in the football world. In a shirt sporting the number used by his former teammate Mark Hughes and shoes custom created to Charlie Miller but was given to him accidentally, David wowed the crowd by taking one of his shots from the midway line, and turned it into an goal. David had seen his opponent Neil Sullivan, the opposing goalkeeper of Wimbledon, stood back from the goal that he was tending from a risky distance. Neil appeared to be anticipating a different approach of Manchester United as the ball was positioned in the mid-way line alongside David and the team of David in the lead by two points. Instead of making an attempt to pass the ball, David took the shot in the shoes with the words "Charlie" and the ball was soaring over Neil and in the goal.

In the Channel 4's UK poll in 2002, the countrymen of David have voted for the above-mentioned goal to be 18th in the 100 Greatest Sporting Moments.

However, prior to the poll was conducted, in the same season David Beckham became Manchester United's most popular player. David Beckham did not disappoint when his contribution to the team helped retain their Premier League Championship. Thanks to his efforts, David was voted by his teammates to be"the" PFA Young Player of the Year.

That identical year David was the first player to make an appearance with the England National Team.

Teammate Eric Cantona retired in May 18, 1997, Eric's highly sought-after shirt number 7 was put to be redeemed. Eric's replacement was Teddy Sheringham, formerly with the Tottenham Hotspurs- David's old team. Beckham handed Teddy the number 10,, while he picked the number 7 for himself. Many supporters were not happy with the decision. Many felt that this number ought to retire along alongside Eric. David didn't seem to mind.

The following season for Manchester United went well but it was not as great than the one before. Because fluctuating performances in the second half of the season, David's squad finished in second place behind Arsenal. But, in 1998-99 The team returned to win with a bang. They won their own Premier League's The Treble, the FA Cup in addition to the Championship League- a very amazing feat in the world of English football.

To ensure they won their Premiere League Title, Manchester United required to win the last game of the season, which was against Tottenham Hotspur. Many reports indicated that Tottenham Hotspur were willing to fall to ensure that their local opponent Arsenal wouldn't be able to keep the trophy. However, this did not turn out as it turned out however, because Tottenham Hotspur took an early advantage during the match. Beckham scored the point. Beckham that scored the goal which was to level the scoring boards, and turn the match in Manchester United's favour.

The price of fame

Beckham's rise to fame did not come with a cost. A lot of critics poured upon Beckham. In spite of the talent David displayed in the course of the season however, he was subject to the nation's fury after being spotted with an intentional foul in the match with Nexaca at the World Cup championship. David received the red card that disqualified him from playing in a match which England ultimately lost. There was speculation that he might move from Manchester United to Juventus to Italy. The truth was that he did not. staying at home in England as well as Manchester United. He had a very valid reasons to. Apart from his devotion to the team that he was raised with the most, a new chapter in his story had begun that could only flourish in the land he grew up in. This chapter will be dubbed by some to be the "Posh and Becks Story".

Chapter 2: Posh And Becks

Victoria's Secret

Victoria Caroline Adams is the second child of Anthony and Jacqueline Adams' three children. Anthony initially worked as an engineer in electronics before establishing his own electronics wholesale company. It allowed him to offer Victoria and her brothers Christian as well as her sister Louise the most comfortable and secure childhood.

At the age of seven, Victoria first saw the Broadway musical Fame in the year 1980 and decided that she wanted to make a profession of the field of music as she got older. Her parents first enrolled her in Jason Theatre School then in Laine Theater Arts in 1991, to learn dancing and modeling.

Victoria attended the Cheshunt's St. Mary's High School for her second year of school. The school was a struggle for Victoria because she was repeatedly bullied and viewed as an outcast by her classmates due to the fact of her wealthy family. Her pleas to her father to not take her to school in his Rolls Royce.

Victory initially tried her hand through music, joining a group called Persuasion. If it didn't go as planned, she enrolled in March 1993, for the advertisement The Stage. Her audition lead her to joining an all-female band called Spice Girls. The group was founded by parents and their management team Bob as well as Chris Herbert. The mid-1990's were when the pop music scene was mostly driven by boys bands such as East 17, West Life and Take That. The marketplace was ready for some new ideas. A girl-only group seemed like an ideal solution. The Spice Girls' first single "Wannabe" hit the airwaves in 1996, it rose immediately to the top spot in both the UK as well as the US along with another 29 other countries.

Victoria was known as "Posh Spice" by the media, and at the time that David Beckham was making waves on the soccer scene. Posh was on top in her field. They first began dating in the month of November, 1996 after Victoria was invited to attend Manchester United in a charity soccer match. The couple were seen regularly in the their public view for nearly three months.

First kiss

David remembers from his autobiography "For the first three months it was amazing because no one found out about us being together. We loved that because we could sneak around. Our first kiss was in the car park of a restaurant. We used to drive to places and just spend as much time together as possible. That was an amazing time in our relationship."

When the public as well as the media spotted their love for each other and their adoration for each other, they were elevated overnight up their place on the A

List. They were media darlings, and the general public gushed over everything they could learn on "Posh and Becks". Their popularity grew because of their habit of attending showbiz events in the same clothes.

On the 25th of January 1998 David fell down to his knees and placed three carats of diamond ring by Boodle and Dunthorpe on Victoria's hand and asked her to marry him. The couple announced their wedding plans and traveled for a romantic trip in Marbella, Spain for a romance-filled holiday.

Victoria did not hesitate to stand by her husband in the event that David received the scorn of the world during the summer of 1998 for getting dismissed during the England's World Cup quarter final battle against Argentina. It was quickly forgotten in the month of March, 1999 they revealed the arrival of their first child Brooklyn. Brooklyn was the name of the baby due to the fact that David as well as Victoria were living in New York when they first discovered they were expecting a baby.

Wedding bells

In the month of July, 1999 they flew together to Ireland for the final time to join in the ceremony. The couple was married at the 5,60-acre Luttrellstown Castle at the Emerald Isle located just outside of Dublin, Ireland. The bride was wearing a elegant champagne colored strapless gown designed by Ivory Vera Wang with a 20-foot train. In her hair, she wore an 18-karat gold crown by diamonds, which was designed by jewelry maker Slim Barrett. David wore an ivory cream-colored suit

The best man in the role was David's teammate Gary Neville and their baby son Brooklyn was Ring bearer. The ceremony was conducted by bishop of Cork Paul Colton. David and Victoria made vows in front of an audience of stars that was comprised of The Spice Girl, David Seaman and Bobby Charlton. One dove, a single white one was released as an emblem of their forever love.

The media were kept out from the wedding because they have agreed to an exclusive contract with OK! Magazine. Newspapers were still in a position to acquire photographs that depicted newlyweds seated on gold the thrones. According to reports, the total of 437 guests were hired to host the wedding reception. The total expense of the event was estimated to be about $800,000.00

The same year, David and Victoria bought a house in Hertfordshire in the amount of PS7.5 million. It was dubbed by the media as"the" Beckingham Palace. The palace was built not too long that their son Brand was born.

Chapter 3: The Gods Of Football Both Scowled And Smiled

Problem with Fergie

The couple began their marriage life by heading straight into work. It was however not an easy path for David. His relationships with Alex "Fergie" Ferguson had started to decline by in the first half of 2000s. It was due to David's success and his involvement which were not directly related to football.

In the year 2000, David was granted the authorization to not attend the practice session at Manchester United in order to take care of his son, who was diagnosed with gastroenteritis. However, Fergie was furious upon seeing the photo of Victoria attending an event sponsored by London Fashion Week sponsored event that was held the same evening as David was absent from the training field. Fergie stated that had Victoria were at home in order to look after the child, David would have made it to training. He Manchester United manager responded by punishing David with a penalty of the limit of PS50,000 (or 2 weeks of pay). Fergie has also sacked David in their crucial match against the opponent Leeds United.

"He was never a problem until he got married. He used to go into work with the academy coaches at night time, he was a fantastic young lad. Getting married into that entertainment scene was a difficult thing - from that moment, his life was never going to be the same. He is such a big celebrity, football is only a small part."' Alex Ferguson said when asked about David's wedding to Victoria.

There were many who previously accused him of having a bad temper. Tabloids also ridiculed his claimed ability to think for himself. David simply reacted to all this with a smile and an affable smile. "You sort of just have to have a sense of humor about it all." He said. "You know, the majority of stuff that is said about me I take with a pinch of salt. When it's about my family or my children, I don't like that. But the majority of stuff that is said about me, you know, I take as a joke, because if you take things too seriously it's going to affect you. Really it would."

Injuries and points

As true as he was to the word he made, David proved his professionalism and was a valuable advantage to Manchester United. David helped Manchester United maintain their title in the Premier League in the 1999-2000 season, with a 18-point advantage despite the performance by Arsenal as well as Leeds United. Manchester United won all the remaining eleven games of the season. David scored five of the six goals in the league for the entire season, and eight goals across every competition.

Furthermore, David Beckham took over the role of Allan Shearer the England's team captain in November 2000, when Shearer quit international football.

In the following season, David Beckham was also the main player to secure Manchester United's third consecutive league win. This was just the fourth time a team has been able to claim three championships within a row. David scored nine goals in the Premier League.

David was injured in April the 10th of April, 2002 he sustained an injury during a game with Deportivo La Coruna for a Champions League game. Second metatarsal bone on Beckham's heel was fractured and speculation was made by media outlets that it was intentionally created by Argentine footballer Aldo Duscher as Argentina as well as England were playing each other in the 2002 World Cup. This is why David did not get to participate for Manchester United for the duration of the campaign. The club lost the Premier League title to Arsenal and also was kicked out of Bayer Leverkusen during the semi-finals.

MU Contract However, David agreed to sign a contract with the club in May of this year following many months of talks and discussions with his club. The main reason behind the delay was the extra fees for Beckham's image-related rights. This, in conjunction the endorsement contracts he signed with firms like Adidas Beckham became the top-earning player on earth in the period. He could manage and get from his team 32,000.00 per week for the image rights by himself. David entered into a lifetime contract with Adidas valued at $ 160 million and was said to be the most lucrative commercial deal in sports history. David also signed an endorsement agreement with Gillette that was worth 10 million dollars in addition to other lucrative agreements.

When he completely recovered David Beckham came back with an enthralling vigor in 2001 and 2002, which was his finest season at Manchester United by scoring eleven goals in the league's 28 games, and 16 goals over all forty-two games in the various competitions. It was without doubt the most impressive total of his entire career.

On September 1, of that same year, David Victoria and David's third baby was born. The couple named him Romeo James. In the same year was an British comedy-drama film that included Keira Knightly, was made and named "Bend It Like Beckham" because of David's amazing ability to score free kicks. He was able to bend the ball in front of the wall of defenders.

The 2002-2003 campaign did not begin well for David. David suffered another injury which kept him from playing within the squad. The left side of the midfield was handed over to Ole Gunnar Solskjaer. In the meantime his relations with his boss Alex Ferguson further deteriorated. On the 15th of February, 2003, when Manchester United lost in an FA Cup game to Arsenal, Fergie threw a boot towards David and it landed on the former on the eye, resulting in a wound that needed stitches. Due to this incident, discussions about Beckham being let go of Manchester United were stirred anew.

But despite the club's poor start Manchester United's performances improved in December, when they were able to win the league. David scored eleven goals over the 52 games played in all contests. Due to this, David is still England's number one selection and later was awarded the Order of the British Empire award for his outstanding performance during the competition on the 13th of June 2003.

David Beckham made 265 games for Manchester United in the Premier League in which he scored sixty-one goals. Beckham also made the 81 Champions League appearances for the squad, where he scored

15 goals. In just twelve years, Beckham had achieved for Manchester United two FA Cups as well as one European Cup and an International Cup as well as one FA Youth Cup. In the same time span, David Beckham was the Manchester United's longest-serving player, only behind Ryan Giggs.

The fame and the endorsements

In the meantime David's popularity had risen to the world beyond his home country. David's name was recognized everywhere because of his endorsement contracts with multinational corporations. It was made possible by the fact that he was married to Victoria who became famous for herself. They were renowned all over the world as a fashion icon and were sought out by a variety of fashion designers for their role as spokespersons, and also magazines and perfume as well as cosmetics producers. An extremely popular scent line and aftershaves that was released to the public was named David Beckham's Instinct. David was also praised as the ultimate metrosexual by Mark Simpson of the magazine The Independent. In fact, it Was Simpson himself who came up with and popularized the phrase in his November 15th 1994 piece for that magazine.

Chapter 4: The Journey From Manchester To Madrid

Real Madrid

As the summer of 2003 was quickly nearing, Manchester United was geared toward selling David Beckham to FC Barcelona. There were announcements made about agreements to move David in to Barcelona. To the dismay of some (and to the chagrin of a few particularly Joan Laporta, the newly elected Barca president who staked his campaign to get David) Beckham instead signed to the current Spanish Champions Real Madrid. Beckham agreed to the sum in the amount of EUR35 million (PS25m) to sign a four-year agreement. The announcement of David's entry to the newly formed Real Madrid roster was first released in the middle of June, but the announcement was not made at the beginning of July. David was the 3rd Englishman to be a part of this Spanish club.

Two of the first two players are Laurie Cunningham and Steve McManaman.

Real Madrid was dubbed as the Yankees of international soccer. The roster of the club included top players such as the French Zinedine as well as Portugal's Luis Figo as well as the Brazilians Roberto Carlos and Ronaldo. David believed he'd blend in perfectly with such skilled players.

The 2nd of July, 2003, following his satisfactory medical examination, David Beckham was presented in front of five hundred journalist from more than 25 countries with a gift from Real Madrid. The event included legend of the club Alfredo di Stefano handing David the Real Madrid shirt with the number 23. David could not take the number 7 as the number at present assigned to team captain Raul. David picked the number 23 based on his respect for the legend basketball player Michael Jordan of the Chicago Bulls and who also wore the number 23 for his jersey.

Beckham isn't the only newcomer for the team. Just a week prior to when David was officially introduced, Real Madrid acquired Carlos Queiroz to become the new team's head coach. David as well as Carlos were previously teammates since Carlos was once an assistant coach for Sir Alex Ferguson for Manchester United.

Changes

When he moved to Spain, David took his entire family in The Spanish capital. Victoria had a difficult time trying to locate a suitable house for her family since she was determined to avoid those extravagant homes which most football players choose to live in. What she was searching for was a house that would be family-friendly.

"You should have seen some of the houses that we saw when we first came out. They were so Hollywood, they had lifts and discos and cinemas and I don't want anything like that. I want something that's a nice size so that, when I'm on my own with the children, I'm not going to feel scared." She told reporters in an interview.

The Beckhams began their lives in an expansive property situated in The La Florida area but eventually they moved to a posh suburb called La Moraleja. David quickly enlisted an instructor to help him get over the difficulty of speaking Spanish. David's Spanish was, of course, initially a bit rough but it did allow him to "understand and communicate" with people in his vicinity.

David had also broken up his relationships with his agent of SFX Europe Tony Stephens. Tony has accompanied David before throughout his career. He even assisted in the relocation of his family to Madrid however David was able to make up his decision. David was signed by Simon Fuller and 19 Entertainment who managed Victoria's career. David was his personal manager. David chose his best buddy Terry Byrne.

Because Spain is a nation that has a culture that is widely known similar to flamenco and bullfighting There was a lot of private space for David Beckham and his family. It was almost impossible for him to stay out of from the attention of others. It didn't deter anyone from attempting. "I think sometimes you've just got to do it," David declares. "I think you have to have some release, where you go out for lunch or dinner and enjoy each other's company no matter what. Sometimes you just have to try to ignore what's going on around you and make the best of it. I'm not one to complain about my life because I realize how lucky I am to be doing what I am doing, to have what I have. It all just comes with the territory."

Asian Tour

In the second half of July 2003 Real Madrid went on a tour of Asia in the course of preparation for the season. The tour was also an opportunity to make money from David's unquestionable appeal as a marketer since David had a huge fan base throughout Asia. Even though Real Madrid was well known throughout The Far East after having made many successful appearances and David's inclusion as a player was a chance they couldn't overlook.

Real Madrid, with David Beckham playing, took home their first Spanish Super Cup in August 2003. They defeated RCD Mallorca in more than two hours. David scored the winner in the victory at home in a match that was three-to-nothing back leg. This was the event that made the difference to begin Real Madrid's journey into the season of league. With famous footballers like Raul, Ronaldo, Luis Figo, Zinadine Zidane and others, it was hard to David to get settled in. David was able to score five times in the first 16 games of the new club, with one of them being the goal he scored just three minutes of his first appearance in La Liga.

Coach Queiroz frequently adapted the 5-3 formation, letting the fullbacks Roberto Carlos and Michel Salgado strike the wings. David was once more able to find his place as a three-man midfielder alongside Zinadine Zidane along with Luis Figo. This formation helped Real Madrid to be one of the runners up in the Copa Del Rey but it did not suffice to earn the trophy for this year's UEFA Championships. The club was knocked out in the quarterfinals of the league and concluded the season fourth in the standings. Real Madrid club president Perez's expectation of either winning or both the Champions League or the Spanish League was thwarted.

The incident did not go down well with the fan base either. The story was that on July 4, 2004, an intruder transporting a gasoline can entered Beckham's residence. Beckham home when David was undergoing preseason training. Victoria and her children were in the house when the incident occurred, but it was a blessing that the intruder was caught before achieving the goal he had set.

The season of the new league began with Real Madrid with a new head coach Jose Antonio Camacho. The only problem was that Camacho was on the team only for three matches. After the team fell to a position of eighth in the league the coach handed in his resignation. Mariano Garcia Remon, his assistant, took temporarily his role as the team's management searched for an appropriate replacement for the position until they came across Lopez Caro.

Play of the foul

It wasn't a very good year for David also since he had a lot of unlucky luck, both in and off the field.

On the 9th of October, 2004, David admitted that in an effort to avoid being arrested, he deliberately hit Ben Thatcher when England went against Wales. David suffered an injury and was slated to be given an one-game suspension that would hinder him from participating at England's next game and, in order to complete the suspension in the game he wasn't taking part in, he committed an intentional foul. The incident did not go down nicely with officials from the Football Association. They had Beckham apologize for his behavior. David acknowledged his error and apologised.

In the league game of Real Madrid in the league match against Valencia CF, David was issued a yellow card. He amused himself by applauding the referee that handed him a yellow card. He received a second yellow card. A second yellow card was the automatic removal of his card. The suspension was lifted the next day after an appeal was filed.

David and Victoria's wedding was not without controversy also. Rumors circulated of David having a relationship and Rebecca Loos, his Madrid-based associate, and the press turned the story a sensation that was described as "the biggest story since Princess Diana's death". After the report was published, Australian model Sarah Marbeck made public her claims that she was also involved in an affair with the soccer player.

In his response, David called the allegations "ludicrous". Victoria supported David however, she later added "I'm not going to lie: it was a really tough time. It was hard for our entire families. But I realized a lot of people have a price." They put their sad moment behind them as well they could. In February of that year, the family was blessed with the arrival of their son, who is the third Cruz. "He's gorgeous, healthy and his mum is very good so we're a very happy family. He's got Victoria's lips and nose," David confidently declared.

But, as of December 2004, Real Madrid was stuck at the bottom of the league. Vanderlei Luxemburgo became the club's new coach, but he failed to assist to win them a trophy because they were forced be content with a runners-up position at the close this season. David himself didn't fare particularly well during his time as coach. The 3rd of December, 2005 David was dismissed for the third time in that season, in their only game with Getafe CF.

David blamed the scandal over his extra marital affairs on his performance the league, as well as during the Euro 2004 championships. He was also blamed for his poor performance at the Euro 2004 championships. England captain's performances were considered not up to par and the country was beaten out of the quarter-final match. This tournament was played shortly after news regarding his reported relationship and Sarah Rebecca as well as Sarah first came out.

The player had categorically claimed that the circumstances were not true. "a lot of things were said about me last season that were not true. Looking back, I can only say that maybe I was taking what was happening on and off the pitch with me in Portugal and that my performance may have suffered slightly."

In 2005-2006 La Liga, Real Madrid was second in the La Liga to FC Barcelona and reached the final 16 only after defeating Arsenal at the Champions League. Perez was removed as the president in January of 2006, in the month of January, and Vicente Bolunda was tagged as an interim replacement until season was over. Ramon Calderon became the new club president in the off-season in summer 2006, and was able to dismiss all former officials under the former president. Coach Lopez Caro was not an the only exception.

The head coach who replaced Fabio Capello as well as David Beckham did not hit the same spot at all. David began only some games during the opening games of the season as the coach Capello prefers Jose Antonio Reyes for the right-wing. Real Madrid lost seven of the initial nine matches Beckham began.

Following a long-running negotiation, Real Madrid sporting director Predrag Mijatovic made the announcement on January 10th the 10th of January 2007 that David Beckham will not remain at the club following the conclusion of the season since his contract was not extended. That same day Beckham declared that he was set to join Los Angeles Galaxy beginning July 1st of 2007 after signing a five-year deal to the organization.

Coach Fabio claimed that David had played his final match with Real Madrid on January 13 in 2007, but he remained to train alongside the team. Calderon was later able to announce in front of a group of pupils that David was "going to Hollywood to be half a film star". Calderon also said that the technical team was correct in not renewing Beckham's contract. Calderon claimed that it was proved by the fact that there was no other technical team around the globe was interested in David apart from Los Angeles Galaxy. In the following year, Capello rescinded his previous remarks about the soccer player and let David to join Real Madrid, just in the time to play in the match against Real Sociedad. David proved to coach Fabio that he could earn the trust of his coach by scoring an equalizer goal off a 27-yard free kick that gave the ball towards Real Madrid. They won two-to-one victory the day.

David was the last player to play in the UEFA Champions League for Real Madrid on the 7th of March 2007. The team was eliminated from the competition when they fell the game to Bayern Munich. Beckham's third match of the Champions League, which placed Beckham in the top three spots on the list of all-time appearances for the tournament.

Money-maker

Beckham had his final match in the final game of his career for Real Madrid on June 17 in 2007, which was the final game in the La Liga Season. The team defeated FC Barcelona and clinched the trophy with a three-to- one score. Beckham was substituted on the pitch with Jose Antonio Reyes when Real Madrid were down by the ratio of zero-1. Reyes had scored the two goals which secured the season's trophy. This was the first time Real Madrid won a title since David who joined the team in 2004 and was their thirty-third overall win throughout the club's history.

Forbes Magazine reported a month following David quit Real Madrid that he was the person to be responsible for the club's dramatic rise in the amount of merchandise sales. According to the report, it was believed that sales had reached around $600 million in David Beckham's time at Real Madrid for four years.

In the final stretch of the season, when David is returned to the good graces of coach Fabio and the team tried to talk to negotiate with LA Galaxy to win Beckham back. However, LA Galaxy put its foot down. David was heading to LA.

Chapter 5: From Madrid To L.A.

Arriving to America

The appearance of David Beckham and his family was initially acknowledged by the reality TV show of one hour Victoria Beckam: Coming to America. The highlight of the program was Victoria's invitation to pitch the very first ball to the Los Angeles Dodgers at a baseball match. When the Beckhams relocated into America, United States, it was quickly apparent that they'd enjoy their new lifestyle living in the United States. They were reported to have said "We love it here. The weather is good and the children are secure. And the main thing is that America is a country where men and women are equal, and the sky's the limit for your career. So I think we'll live here for a while."

They acquired an Italian Villa located in San Ysidro Drive, Beverly Hills with a value of around 22 million dollars with a view of the city. It was near to the home of talk show anchor Jay Leno and thespians Tom Cruise and Katie Holmes.

As part of the deal in the transfer to LA Galaxy, David was mentioned on the July cover of The Sports Illustrated Magazine. The cover was released a couple of months before Adidas released a massive campaign featuring David titled "Futbol matches Football. David and his wife also appeared on the cover of W Magazine. The picture's title referred to the management firm that manages David as well as Victoria and also the relationship between the company's founder to American Idol. The same company also produced a documentary on television produced by Gary Brooks entitled "David Beckham"A New Beginning". The show aired just prior to when David took to the stage for the American debut at a friendlies game against Chelsea.

There were many concerns raised prior to when David was able to make the American debut. Many had questioned how he could improve the game that was not so popular in his homeland of England. Beckham was asked this question. Beckham responded "I'm coming there not to be a superstar. I'm coming there to be part of the team, to work hard and to hopefully win things. With me, it's about football. I'm coming there to make a difference. I'm coming there to play football ... I'm not saying me coming over to the States is going to make soccer the biggest sport in America. That would be difficult to achieve. Baseball, basketball, American football, they've been around. But I wouldn't be doing this if I didn't think I could make a difference".

David's agreement began to take effect on the 11th of July, 2008 David was the latest player to join LA Galaxy two days later in the Home Depot Center in front of a crowd comprised of 735 accredited media professionals and five thousand supporters. David chose to wear the exact jersey number that he wore during his time at Real

Madrid, 23. The announcement was made as a matter of fact that after David's official introduction his official debut, sales of Galaxy jerseys had set the record amount of 250,000 within a small amount of time.

LA Galaxy Team Captain

Beckham was then made the new captain of the team. To prove that he's worthy of the awards and praises given to the new team by his former team, David made his Galaxy debut on the 21st of July the 21st of July, 2008 in spite of an injury to his ankle that he suffered one month prior to that with Real Madrid. The fan base for the game, which was a friendly match against Chelsea during the World Series of Soccer was attracted by Hollywood stars such as Alicia Silverstone, Jennifer Love-Hewitt, Eva Longoria, Mary-Kate Olsen Drew Carey, Arnold Schwarzenegger, Tom Cruise and Katie Holmes. ESPN broadcast the match live on their main channel. Even with the presence of soccer stars such as Michael Ballack, John

Terry and Didier Drogba, cameras were all on David all the time although he was spending the majority of the match on the bench.

Beckham was not the only player to get anxiety during the game they were defeated by Chelsea by a score of zero-to-one when he was smashed by Steve Sidwell. The cleats that Sidwell threw at David's foot, sending him flying into the ground, screaming in the pain. The previous injury did not severe, but it caused him to delay his recovery by one month.

The Beckhams received a second welcome party in the Los Angeles Museum of Contemporary Art on the same day. It is believed that the event was had been hosted by Hollywood celebrities Will Smith, Jada Pinkett Smith, Tom Cruise and Katie Holmes however it was actually CAA who arranged the event. It was attended by number of celebrities from Hollywood and received coverage from the US celebrities' media, including E!, Access Hollywood and Entertainment Tonight.

Chapter 6: The Beckham Galaxy Traveling With David

Much to the annoyance of his supporters, David missed four of LA Galaxy's games. Three of them included the North American Super Liga and one of them was at Toronto FC. Beckham went to Canada together with the rest of his teammates and sat down on benches in his streetwear. It was Toronto for the LA Galaxy players when LA Galaxy got a taste of what it's as it was to travel in the same place as David.

Due to safety issues Due to safety concerns, the team took an unscheduled flight rather than taking a commercial flight at first. Charter flights for far-flung games were generally not permitted in Major League Soccer. However, since David tends to cause huge fanfare around himself so they needed to be able to get around this. They were also not placed in the typical MLS-mandated hotel rooms. Instead, they had to live in a 5 star hotel Le Meridien King Edward.

It was nearly two weeks since David had made his first appearance with LA Galaxy. David was not fully recovered, but he made his debut for the league at RFK arena on August 9th, 2007, in a replacement role for the game against DC United in front of an audience that was three times more than the typical DC United home crowd. David was substituted for Quavas Kirk during the match's initial seventy minutes, despite the torrential downpour, leaving the team was down by a goal but not a man. For the remaining 20 minutes, he scored an open goal that was missed by his teammate Carlos Pavon failed to convert for an equalizer. Pavon then served the ball through, but was blocked by DC United's goalkeeper Troy Perkins.

David was forced to miss in the next game with the New England Revolution because he was afraid of further injury to his ankle because they were playing at Gillette Stadium which had an artificial turf.

The 15th of August, 2007 David was on the field a week following his New England Revolution match for another encounter in the semi-finals against DC United for the semi-finals of Super Liga. This was a game that was full of firsts for David. It was his debut game as the newly appointed captain of the team, and also being the first time he scored an assist and the first time an assist was successful to Landon Donovan during the second quarter, as well as his first time receiving an yellow card in his time playing with LA Galaxy. LA Galaxy won the game with a 2 to one victory, earning the right to play in the final against Pachuca on the 29th of August to play in the North American Super Liga.

Further accidents

The Super Liga finals versus Pachuca David's right knee became injured. A MRI scan found a ruptured medial collateral ligament. It meant he'd be out of action for the next six weeks. However, Beckham returned on the field to take part in the final game of the season. The 21st of October LA Galaxy was eliminated from the play-offs for the MLS finals, in a game against Chicago Fire. David was a substitute in the game, scoring the eighth game for his newly formed team, scoring the scoring of one goal with three assists.

Like every other time, problems outside the football field was also an issue for David Beckham. The bodyguard and he were suing Emicles de Mata, a photographer for paparazzi who claimed that he was assaulted by two as he tried to capture a photograph of Beckham's footballer at Beverly Hills. The photographer demanded an unspecified amount of damages in the case of assault, battery and the intentional trauma to the emotional.

Three weeks from the 4th of January, 2008 David Beckham trained with Arsenal and then returned with LA Galaxy for pre-season training. David Beckham scored his debut club goal on the 3rd of April in the 9th minute in their match in the match against San Jose Earthquakes. LA Galaxy defeated Kansas City Wizards following a three to one match on the 24th of May on May 24, the 24th of May, 2008. David got an unmarked goal from a seventy yard line. It was only the second occasion in his career the goal was scored at such a distances within his own half. The club got the first win over the past two seasons and helped propel to the top position in the Western Conference. But, LA Galaxy failed to be able to qualify for the final season play-off.

Chapter 7: Here And Back

David Beckham's 2008 success as England's captain together with Fabio Capello has sparked speculation that David was set to return to Europe for a second time to keep his performance for 2009 World Cup Qualifying matches. The rumors were even granted the chance to renew his contract after AC Milan announced that Beckham will join them being on loan until January 2009. However, David stated that he has no plans to quit MLS and that the club would allow him to return LA Galaxy just in time for the start of the 2009 season which is scheduled to begin in March.

AC Milan

There was not a single person in AC Milan was ready to simply accept Beckham's appearance for the moment. Some footballers saw it as an unintentional marketing strategy. David selected the number 32 on the AC Milan jersey. The number was used previously for Christian

Vieri. The numbers 7 and 23 had previously been utilized in the past by Alexandre Pato and Massimo Ambrosini.

David's first appearance with Milan took place on the 11th of January of 2009, against Roma to play the Serie A match. David lasted 90 minutes during the game that ended with the draw. The 25th of January David scored his first strike on Serie A for his temporary team, in a 4-1 one victory over Bologna. Beckham made his third time playing for AC Milan. Following scoring goals in his first four games and helping in a few additional goals, AC Milan was so amazed by the performance of David that they decided to give Beckham a spot in the squad. However, AC Milan was unable to beat LA Galaxy's estimate of David's footballer in the ten-to-15 million US dollar price range.

But, AC Milan would not be a slouch at the negotiations table. In March, it was revealed that David's transferred to Milan was extended until the middle of July in a unique "time share" deal where Beckham could play with LA Galaxy from the middle of July to the close of 2009's MLS season.

"Go home fraud"

When he returned back to LA Galaxy, a lot of unhappy fans mocked David Beckham for missing half of the season. They hung up signs that stated "Part Time Player" and "Go Home Fraud". David did not hesitate to laugh at them and explained that two teams were competing to see his abilities on the field. David was a crucial player in the team of LA Galaxy and helped them to win victory in the 2009 Western Conference final in a defeat of two-to-none against Houston Dynamo. LA Galaxy lost in the final game to Real Salt Lake in the last game on November 22, 2009, by five-4 during a penalty shootout which resulted from drawing one and only. David scored during the shootout.

LA Galaxy had had a better season when they had David as their coach in comparison to the previous seasons. They went from being third in the league to second on the Western Conference with Beckham's help.

In the final stages of 2009's MLS Season, David returned to AC Milan in November 2009 to sign a loan for another one that will begin in January. Beckham returned to form an incredible return in AC Milan on January 6 with a seventy-five minute match against Genoa and securing an impressive five to two win. The 16th of February David Beckham played against his previous club Manchester United in San Siro in his first game since having left them in 2003. David was on the pitch for seventy-six mins prior to being substituted to Clarence Seedorf .The game ended with a 3-2 score to Manchester United.

On the 10th of March, 2010 David Beckham was again at Old Trafford for the second part of the match. Beckham was not part of the first line-up and was substituted sixty-four minutes after the match for Ignazio Abate. The score was 3 to one and the match was pretty much resolved. It was the first time that David was playing against Manchester United wherein he created many scoring opportunities with corners kicks and crosses. Manchester United still dominated AC Milan with a four-to- none final score. They also ended the match with a seven-to-two.

David was then a player with AC Milan in a game against Chievo Verona. In this game, Beckham was injured by a ruptured the left Achilles tendon. It caused him to miss the MSL season, as well as his participation in the World Cup since he needed 5 months to repair the wound.

Following David recuperated, David was back at LA Galaxy and played on the 11th of September game, as a substitute for the seventh minute. LA Galaxy won that game against Columbus Crew with a three one goal score. In the following months after, he scored an iconic free kick in a 2-0 to one win against Chivas. The goal was his first in 2010. He added his second goal on October 24, in the two-to-one win against Dallas and helped secure for LA Galaxy their second successive Western Conference title. Also, he helped the team to win the debut MLS Supporters Shield.

Between January and February of 2011, Beckham trained with Tottenham Hotspurjust a few months in advance of 2011, the MLS season. The news spread that Tottenham Hotspur were in talks with LA Galaxy to sign the footballer for a loan. These rumors weren't unfounded but the possibility of a realization was stopped through LA Galaxy, which wanted David to play the full season. David did end up working for the Tottenham Hotspur like he did Arsenal.

MLS Championship

The year 2011 was the one which gave LA Galaxy their first MLS Championship cup, which was won by David Beckham. David Beckham scored his first goal of the season on an unintentional free kick from thirty yards during a 4-1 victory over Sporting Kansas City. On the 9th of July, he scored straight from an unorthodox corner kick in an all-square win against Chicago Fire. Similar to what he did during their match in the match against Preston North End.

David completed his fifth season playing for the MLS with a dazzling performance. In the end, it was his most successful season at LA Galaxy and he finished 2nd in league assists. He became part of a elite group of players who had been crowned champions in three tournaments across three nations on the 20th of November 2011. LA Galaxy won the MSL Cup first time following a win against Houston Dynamo. It was a the one-to-none ratio thanks to the score of Landon Donovan with assists from Robbie Keane and David

Beckham. If this was David's final game for the club it would be the third time that he has won the league championship during his last match with a club. It was the first time at Manchester United in 2003 and another in 2007 with Real Madrid in 2007.

Chapter 8: Still Kickin And Even After The Field

New contract

It was a wonderful moment in the life of David Beckham. Apart from winning playing in the MSL Cup, LA Galaxy were crowned the winner of the Supporter's Shield two times in succession which was the second-highest numbers of points in time of Major League Soccer. David's contract was up on December 31, 2011. However, his time on the stadium were not ending. Even though he was 36 years old, the age of his player, he declared that his retirement is not complete yet. In this regard, the news was released on day, January 18, 2012 that David has signed an agreement to LA Galaxy that will let the club play through 2014.

His relationship with Victoria is as solid like ever. The couple were frequently seen together along with their kids in Hollywood playing basketball or taking their dogs for walks. They were also observed watching shows or together with famous families that included the rocker Gwen Stefani.

David and Victoria have celebrated their 13th anniversary wedding on the 14th of July in 2012. "We are as in love, if not more in love, than ever," declared Victoria. "We are best friends. We never put pressure on each other. It was our 11th wedding anniversary at the weekend and we celebrated it in style... It was a fabulous party."

As David examines his past at his past, he realizes that he never planned to get married to the biggest pop stars or to have a chat with celebrities and own sprawling estates in different parts of the world and drive luxury cars or wear extravagant clothes and jewels. What he really wanted was an elite football player. Today, he's living his dreams, and the rest of his life was only perks from his success in his game.

Charities

The idea of giving to others is, therefore, not an uncommon thought for David Beckham. Many may view Beckham as just another high-paying Hot-headed, exuberant jock who hit the jackpot. Given all the gossip which had plagued him for all over the years, it could be difficult to help. However, many people do not realize that he was a supporter of UNICEF from the beginning of his football career with Manchester United. Then, in January 2005, he became an ambassador for Goodwill of UNICEF with a particular focus in the organization's Sports for Development Program. He also had pledged his to support the cause Unite for Children, Unite Against Aids.

He also serves as the spokesperson of a New York City-based non-profit known as Malaria No More. The group was founded in 2006 has embarked working to prevent death due to the illness. In 2007 David was featured on the air in a public service advertisement that promoted the need for cheap mosquito nets.

When he joined Major League Soccer, he began to be a highly active advocacy advocate across the United States for charities related to the soccer league, such as MLS W.O.R.K.S.

On the 17th of August 17, 2007 David was the host of a youth camp held in Harlem, New York along with current and former players from MSL. The footballers along with him gave sports skills lessons to young people who are in need.

One person who saw the heart underneath the pro-footballer/rock star exterior of David Beckham is Rebecca Johnstone who is a 19-year cancer sufferer living in Hamilton, Ontario Canada. The two never had a personal meeting however Rebecca received a surprising phone message from her soccer hero and, following their chat,

David sent her a autographed Real Madrid jersey.

In the present, David Beckham remains one of the biggest sports stars and could continue as such in the future. It's an understatement to say that he'd made a significant progress since playing soccer when he was a kid at Ridgeway Park and becoming not only one of the most highly valued and most sought-after players in the world, as well as one of the best known brands and endorsers. In the press, it was said that David wasn't the heir to the British throne. He was said to be far more. They claimed he was a rock star sporting an soccer shirt. Rock star wearing a soccer gear with a generous heart. A loving family who remains his main the source of his strength both at and off the pitch.

Chapter 9: The Little Red Devil

Robert Joseph Beckham was born on May 2in 1975 at Leytonstone, Essex. Even though it's within the boundaries of Essex, Leytonstone has its own tube station, which provides rapid accessibility to London and is considered to be an integral part of the urban sprawl. David was born into an ordinary, working-class family: his father Ted worked as a gasfitter while his mother Sandra was a hairdresser. David was born to two sisters: Lynne as well as Joanne.

Leytonstone was a football fanatic like any other player within the London region. Ted had, for a while, hopeful that he would be able to make an illustrious career playing football.

He was not able to have the edge that separates professional players, even though the local leagues he played for when he could. It was unique in the sense that he didn't support Leyton Orient, the local team and neither did he support West Ham, the big East London team.

The man was a vilified type of football fan with loyalties extending far from home: Manchester United or, as it is referred to colloquially and phonologically, ManU. Ted to the chagrin of his father who was an Arsenal fan became enthralled by the team from Matt Busby. United certainly had a glamor which other teams didn't possess, but by the time David became a boy, the club was at a low point. The team had just recently re-emerged their team from the second division after struggling in adjusting to life following Busby.

David was two years old. David was a mere two and struggling to concentrate on the TV screen, United won their first domestic title for the tenth time in a row winning against the great Liverpool at the 1997 FA Cup Final, which brought back interest in the team which was now run by an energetic Scot, Tommy Docherty.

They made it to the final the following year and were now playing they were under Dave Sexton after Tommy Docherty quit the club because of a sexual assault scandal. They fell in that final however by the time they lost, David was already a United fan, enthralled by his father's passion and eager to watch the team in action.

When David was five years old, the day finally arrived, the day that Ted brought him along for a visit to see United perform at Spurs the other family-friendly club. It was a moment that will be remembered in both of their lives. The two had to travel with Ted around lunchtime in his older Ford Escort van to get to the stadium before the masses, and David was dressed in his United tracksuit, and was brimming with joy at the thought of watching people such as Steve Coppell, Stewart Houston and Gordon McQueen.

The match itself, an uncontested draw unfortunate to be a symptom of the momentous United team. Dave Sexton was a respected soccer coach, but wasn't known for his flair for attacking as evidenced by the book that he wrote about the game dubbed TTaacckkllee Socccerr. United

Fans, who were bloodied by the cheers during players like the Busby Babes, were frequently indignant about the sloppy football that his teams played and players often became distracted due to his slick way of instructing.

For a five-year old boy sitting in the very first moment at an actual football stadium, to watch the squad of his dreams there were no objectives and was a true spectacle which he will remember for the rest of his existence. The moment he was transported through the turnstiles, to the initial scream of the official's whistle, his excitement grew. Early arrivals created more drama as the stadium gradually grew larger until it was completely packed with just five minutes remaining before kickoff.

He screamed in delight while the United team rushed onto the field, and Ted has never been more excited. Even though Ted was an experienced spectator, the match went by without a trace for the kid. Once the event was complete and Ted took the tired youngster across the turnstiles he realized that the event was evidently enthralled his son.

The man told him: 'One day, I'm going to be a player for Manchester United.'

The father said"I'll watch you, even if you're playing with Barnet.'

David was a sports enthusiast and skilled at whatever the opportunity presented itself, however the game of football as well as Manchester United became his overriding love. The greatest heroes of his included Bryan Robson and Mark Hughes The two greatest players from the current Ron Atkinson era at United the walls of his bedroom were adorned with pictures of them in order to match his United bedsheet, pillowcase and curtains.

Ted had started to play an object around in the yard and whenever the time came to go to junior school, it was common for him to take a ball to school every single day, even if it was two minutes walk. In time, Ted realized that he was born with an extraordinary talent for soccer even the smallest of players will recognize the obvious indicators. Because Ted did not make the required level so he started doing it by his son. He started coaching his son on an advanced level even though David was already practicing regularly at his own.

He'd train for hours at the outdoor area, throwing the ball against the wall and controlling the ball instantly, focusing at his instep and turning it onto his chest, before transferring it to the thighs and then returning to the head. He would be doing these boring drills, but the fundamental individual abilities were soon becoming automatic, and Ted taught him his technique of using the ball to aid in helping the team score goals but not to concede goals.

David's parents Ted Beckham and Sandra Beckham

Ted was playing local game, but shortly David began to ask him to join in with fully grown males. This was his first glimpse that showed the strength of him and his unwavering attitude of his teammates contributed to his toughness. Dad told me later: "A few times, I would say: "All right, come to the field now. However, don't try to hold the ball, because when you did, you're likely be caught in a clump."'

There were three or four times that He was knocked to the ground and then walked away from the field crying. I was like "See what I mean?" It was a good thing for him as the fact that he could learn quickly.'

He was such a swift learner that, soon instead of seeing him as a Ted's child that made up the numbers, they began engaging him in the game. Just like any other player there were his down times; his dad was forced to "bawl" his son out' and bring David in tears two instances. It was a great learning encounter, also because David would be meeting the coach in the future, who was tougher than his father The coach was adamant about balancing harsh criticism with warm compliments.

It would become a very uncommon sight to find David Beckham without a football. Beckham only joined his Boy Scouts, for instance as football was among the main actions. On weekends and after school, David either headed to the park to play with his friends or played an event in the youth league. When he was eight years old the young man joined Ridgeway Rovers of the Enfield District League which quickly transformed into the most famous player of the club and goal scorer. His agility, speed and control of the game were all very impressive in his day It was during this time that the beginning of the thousands photographs taken of David Beckham in action came to be taken.

The famous photo of the boy with spiky hair (but sporting the characteristics we recognize today are already obvious to notice) with a grimace on his face. His eyes appear less than the ball which he's kicking. At an early stage, he showed an extremely robust right foot that soccer scouts who were hovering around him marked on their minds as worthy of more attention. He could strike the ball with incredible force considering his size and age and more the public could clearly see his ability of curving his passes and shots with finesse and precision which was not often seen during those times, even in senior levels.

The ball's bend is being taught in the schools at a young age, but it is also an acknowledgement of the impact Beckham's style of play had an impact on English football. A reliance too heavily on power, strength and tempo at all levels in the English game is a grass roots disadvantage that still restricts development. This can be seen in the many international players that arrive on this country with the abilities which allow them to excel within the chaos of the Premiership. But there are there are few homegrown players who can do similar things in the world.

It was the Graham Taylor era, when Carlton Palmer, a bungling midfielder who was the first to be listed in the England roster and was a high point of the aforementioned malaise. Graham Taylor's major contribution to the sport was to introduce park football into the international scene. It is also forgotten as fans still bemoan the fact that they remember his achievements, namely that he gained more points than he did lose. Naturally, the speedy and frantic Route One football can and can win games against better-trained, fluid teams. When a large number of fifty-50 balls are made in the 18-yard area fast, powerful players who shoot effectively and who are skilled on the ground will be able to score scores. In addition, as the players for the English game have reminded us it is the goal that defines the game. of the game, and it isn't a matter of how you get they will be scored.

It could be reduced to a question of whether football is 'a man's sport' or "the gorgeous game'. For the former, the game as a contest in which manhood will be tested while the latter see it is what an alternative England director, Ron Greenwood, once said, "want to experience enjoyment on the field as well as joy on the fields. . .'

It is true that there is an inconsistency of opinion regarding these two ways of playing the game. It all is a matter of your personal taste and preferences. However, there's a minor difficulty with the idea that, at the top level the English game is not a good idea to put its silverware on display in the cabinet.

Beckham's tastes and choices were always in the direction of art, not combat. In addition to his ManU admirers, his favorite player was also a member of Spurs. Glenn Hoddle was one of the finest technically proficient players of his generation having a variety of passes and shooting that appeared completely inappropriate for the English sport.

Hoddle's Tottenham teammate Garth Crooks has often recalled his experiences receiving the passes of Hoddle when the ball dropped directly in front of him, and then was thrown backwards upon contact with turf straight to his way. In the rare occasions Hoddle was a player for England and the United States, he would bring this kind of talent together, which included the unbelievable ability to bend an unintentional kick around an obstacle. It was one of the talents which David determined to develop into his own.

David became stronger and appeared better than ever and his passion for playing didn't decrease. Although he was a proficient student, and he worked quite well, all things was put aside for football. He began equipping himself with the most advanced equipment available. As he grew older and had enough money, he began taking on odd jobs to make extra income. One of his most memorable jobs was collecting empty glass bottles at the Walthamstow dog park.

Chapter 10: Together With Bobby Charlton

Ted and Sandra made sure their son was kept to a certain standard by utilizing the sport's popularity as a carrot and a stick. In the event of a mishap, they'd keep him from playing and there was no thing he was more resentful of than his parents. Then he was the focus of a fierce recruitment fight between several clubs. He was a player for Essex Schools and Leyton Orient as well as attended Tottenham

The Hotspur school of Excellence. Tottenham specifically attempted to lure him and his father by offering free tickets to games (which they refused to turn down!) But the red and black of United was evident in his veins.

The representatives from Manchester began to express interest in. The dream was realized by the rest of his life when He kicked a ball in Old Trafford in December 1986 at the age of 11. He was chosen to go to at the Bobby Charlton Soccer Schools from 1986-1988, and was able to pass the Skills Assessments. He won the top position with his coach group and was selected to compete in the National Skills Final, also which was held in Old Trafford.

David was up against 100 other contestants from all over the UK and Ireland. David won the competition with a score of 1,100 marks, with his closest rivals coming in just below four numbers. The reward for winning his place in the Bobby Charlton National Skills final was a week-long trip to FC Barcelona, where he was able to meet next England director Terry Venables and Barcelona players like former Manchester United player Mark Hughes. The school's coach, Bryn Cooper, has described the incredible growth of David as a player in the early days David was a phenomenal athlete in his early years. David had amazing abilities as young man. The age group of this year was the class of 14+. However, David still achieved the most impressive score for his skills among the students. The result was sufficient to persuade Bobby Charlton for one, as well as his guidance, David was offered the possibility of becoming an Manchester United trainee in 1991.

It was a thrilling moment for the 16-year old who had fulfilled an ardent desire - however, the association he had with Manchester United did not come at an appropriate moment. When he walked out his way to the Old Trafford pitch for the first time, Manchester United were still welcoming a new coach, Alex Ferguson. The previous manager, Ron Atkinson had presided over two FA Cup victories but the United board favored League title more. Moreover the team finished fourth in the season, having begun as favorites and sounded like losing the following year, Atkinson was shown the entrance.

The former Aberdeen manager Ferguson was the man who transformed a mediocre

Scottish team into a European strength, took over from Atkinson an unsavory chalice. The team had a genuine top player and captain be sure of in one David's most famous players Bryan Robson, but the entire team was thought to be extremely unstable. The moment that Ferguson was seated at his desk in the early days, even though United were among the richest teams in Britain but they were third to last in the former First Division and relegation looked an actual possibility.

Ferguson was also worried some of the players were consuming too much (for all the glory he showed at the field, Bryan Robson was a drinker) and was "depressed over their state of fitness. But, with his typical determination, he was able to boost the discipline of his players and United made a comeback and finished the season in the 11th position.

Ferguson signed several key players during the 1987/88 season which included Steve Bruce, Viv Anderson,

Brian McClair and Jim Leighton. These newcomers significantly improved the team, and they came in second but still nine points back of Liverpool. United were not expected to be successful after Mark Hughes, another of David's idols, joined United, but the 1988-89 campaign was an unfulfilling experience for them and they finished 11th in the league. They also lost 1-1 at home against Nottingham Forest in the FA Cup quarterfinal. In the season of 1989, under pressure Ferguson hired two new midfielders as well as a central defender to increase his odds for success during the 1989-90 season. In the first game of the season United defeated the champions of the past Arsenal 4-1. There was an expectation that the league crown that was lost since 1967 was coming back in Old Trafford. However, in September United were hammered 5-1 in an away loss to the rivals Manchester City. It was not a great year, and by the month of November Old Trafford witnessed a banner that read: "Three years of excuses and the result is still a mess. "Ta ra Fergie!

It was a dark time for Ferguson however he persevered and won his beloved FA Cup back to the club in the year 1990. Following the season, in which David was a student he was crowned his first European Cup Winners' Cup Final in the final against Barcelona however United remain a massive dismal at the top of the table. Even though they had the European award, the team were lagging behind the league leaders in sixth position, then a year after that, they lost everything away in the final three games. There was a chance that league glory could not be achieved for the Reds.

In this moment, David was settling down like many other players older than him, he adapted quite well from his home. David was determined to embark on a professional life and loved playing soccer so much that having to be away from the family for days or weeks in a row did not bother his. He was drafted into the ManU's youth squad and was able to meet at first, talent like Ryan Giggs, Paul Scholes, Nicky Butt and Gary Neville who would become his greatest friend.

With Ferguson watching proudly with pride, they were the main players in the team who won the FA Youth Cup in 1992 and symbolized the future of United. Ferguson was very protective of the young ones and believed it was a good thing David was good enough to be promoted to United's first team during the month of October in the following season. During the second round of the league cup (then the Rumbelows Cup) he came to the substitute position in place of Andrei Kanchelskis, then United's legendary right midfielder

The season was a pivotal moment in the club's fortunes. Ferguson has an inconsistent record on the transfer market, yet possessing a sharp sense of a player Ferguson struck one of his best moves.

The club enticed French forward Eric Cantona from Leeds for PS1 million. This was one player that could strike a soccer ball with a sweet touch: Cantona combined with Mark Hughes to lead United to their first win in their 26-year history.

A new period of unparalleled achievement began at the club just the time David tried to get his name out of the ring.

Ferguson was a plethora of midfield options, and David did not play in any first-team matches for the whole 1993-94 season. The player was enraged as his team sailed to yet another League triumph, which was boosted by the signing to Roy Keane who was the perfect, long-term replacement for

David at Preston

Bryan Robson. Bryan Robson. Lee Sharpe and Ryan Giggs playing alongside Kanchelskis on the flanks the new season kicked off but there is no evidence of David having the ability to make himself into the squad.

Youngsters only had their chances when the seniors fell short in the Champions League, and 19-year-old David had his first taste of European game action during the 4-0 victory against Galatasaray during December 1994. He scored, but due to the other games going against United the previous week, this was dead rubber in the end.

In the early months of 1995, David received an explosive news item and his father got a frantic phone message from the child"Dad. The boss is asking me to go out in loans to Preston. Is that right? I'm not sure whether they dislike me. I'm sure they're trying to rid me of them I'm sure they do,' he snorted. "He said that it will benefit me and help me become stronger. He told me I could play there for a few games, and continue to train at United on a week-long basis. In spite of his concerns about his son's future in the club United, Ted was far-sighted enough to realize that it was a wise decision by Fergie's side, and in a way of offering his son first-team experience in addition to acclimatising him to the rigors that come with the Premiership. Ted further insisted on would actually make the move to Preston in the knowledge that players from the top would be grudging if he showed on for games, yet wasn't able to join their training. This was an intelligent decision.

The time was only a short time however David quickly realized that playing competitively regardless of the level was vital to his progress. Preston director Gary Peters welcomed David with full arms. And when everyone else in the team were aware that he wasn't the primo donna, they welcomed him as well. When he first played for the team, David scored direct from an angle. Actually, he performed so well during his subsequent four matches that, he did not know the club - United had been thinking about taking him off the team.

However, Peters was delighted by the development of young David in the short amount of time, and was keen to remain until the conclusion this season. David seemed to have decided that this would be another year that United will not want the player, so he wanted to stay to stay, but he had to talk with Ferguson to discuss his decision. It was an incredibly stressful experience even for a player who was incredibly hard-core as very few players in the game are as passionate like Ferguson's.

Beckham was also well-aware of his involvement in the recent United legends. Beckham's teammate from his FA Youth Cup squad, Ryan Giggs, had just made it into the first-team group when he became taken advantage of in a vicious humorous joke played from Bryan Robson and Steve Bruce.

They enticed the incredulous Giggs that he was able to request for a car from the club as a reward for his standing as a senior footballer. Giggs then went to Ferguson's office to submit his request. He was then metaphorically attacked by the help of a Gatling because of his petty annoyances.

Young David asked for something reasonable in comparison to the other players, yet it's still a rather naive event to knock on the door of the manager first time. Ferguson's reaction was about exactly the same way as when Giggsy fell. Ferguson slammed his fist into the desk and yelled "You're not going to be a good sport going any where. Staying here is fucking good which is the last word of the story.' David was completely surprised, but he realized better than to fight so he turned around and left the office in a state of confusion.

The man was as he had been when the man moved

beyond the warning

board will be available later

And discovered the cause of the manager's

fury. Ferguson kept an eye on him

On David while he was on sabbatical Preston

More than he realized that his progression had been

The reward was that he was listed in the teamsheet of the

Next game is the following game against Leeds. He called Ted to inform him of the

The news he received:

'I'm playing, Dad. . .I'm with the squad

to play tomorrow's match in the game tomorrow against Leeds.

I'm my dad, that's the truth . . . I'm living in the

squad!'

The 1994/95 season could have been a

It was a difficult game difficult one Manchester United, it was

One that saw David slowly working

his place in the manager's head in the role of an

An alternative in place of Andrei Kanchelskis, who was

being afflicted with suffering from. The situation is typical for Fergie.

management style, which he used to do was evident when David screamed David

He never explained to his father why, he just to let him

find out for himself. They are like livestock.

Fergie and he's also the herder. He was once the player's

The yield is below the level of championship He is

sold. The sale was not only for Andrei Kanchelskis in

the risk of losing his spot at the back, however

Midfield enforcement Paul Ince was playing his

Last season was a good one for United also.

The husbandry principle should not allow anyone to feel any emotion, but Fergie is only human. So if Fergie doesn't enjoy the player well, he'll eliminate his player (Jaap Stam) and then he'll join forces with "rogue" players, particularly if there is a negative press reaction. But, of course, their performance should be still good. The big name players could be just as unpredictable as they are skilled. Thus, players like Roy Keane and Eric Cantona (who is currently being suspended for kicking as a Crystal

Palace fan) attract an especially passionate and steady defense. Beckham could one day find reasons to be thankful for the stoic attitude of his manager.

Cantona's craziness was just one of many downs in the season in which they fell in the Premiership against Blackburn during the Premiership but lost the title on the last day the season. Ferguson was able to take action to ensure it didn't happen again however, he received a lot of smears in 1995's summer after three of the club's most coveted players were relegated and replacements were not purchased. In the first instance, Paul Ince moved to Inter Milan at a cost of PS7 million. Within just 24 hours after Ince's departure, Mark Hughes was suddenly sold to Chelsea for a bargain PS1.5 million contract. The shock was that it was revealed that he had not signed the contract that he was offered in month of January. Then, Andrei Kanchelskis was packed away to Everton in exchange for PS5 million. This deal was the one that suited David the most.

However, Fergie has backed himself in a corner intentionally believing that he could have a lot of youngsters who were able to step into the squad and succeed.

The youngsters who were referred to as "Fergie's Fledgings', comprised those from the Nevilles, Paul Scholes, Nicky Butt. . . And David Beckham or Becks as the team members called him by name.

The team was defeated in its initial match of the following season by 3-1 against Aston Villa, Ferguson came into the spotlight for a lot of criticism. Some sections of the media were swooping in glee. MMaattcchh Ooff TTHHEE DDaayy Pundit Alan Hansen famously proclaimed 'you will never win anything when you have kids However, Hansen played at Liverpool. However, the majority of commentators discredited

Fergie's youthful team and bookmakers even gave odds of relegation.

Becks was among the few bright spots during the 3-1 loss. He scored the team's sole goal which was the top of all four and his first time in the Premiership. The tide appeared to have changed as United were victorious in their subsequent five matches. David appeared to be confident at the right side of the field and his quality passing and shooting was clear to observe. In the wake of Ferguson buying an erratic player Andy Cole from Newcastle for huge sums of money in the past He needed a player capable of serving up opportunities in a mug. Beckham fit the bill. Beckham quickly built trust with Old Trafford fans, who were impressed by his talents but also his incredible efficiency.

David was transforming into an athlete. He's not the best tackler or an athlete of speed, however he is hard to get past and covers a huge amount of space. On average the team estimated that to be running around eight miles in 90 minutes. This is greater than most athletes.

Chapter 11: Kevin Keegan

Beckham was one of the latest generation of footballers that focused on their overall fitness levels: he was properly trained and there was not any burning candles in the middle, particularly on both sides. A time in which players like Tony Adams at Arsenal - who later admitted that he had an alcohol addiction was able to continue his addiction and his professional career had ended. Paul Gascoigne's case is also an awakening. The man who would eventually become England's greatest footballer had, at least for a moment an actual professional athlete.

In his defense, after he was appointed manager of Manchester United Alex Ferguson quickly recognized that the club's alcohol culture was undermining the record of silverware won by the club. The legends and addicts such as Paul McGrath (a Red from 1982 to 1989) represented the stale image of the club. Fergie insists on a certain level of fitness and physical strength that kept players away from alcohol or women as well as song.

David's temptations arose while he was out of the Fergie regime by being in the call-up for England and sociable with such celebrities as Tony Adams and Gazza. Even were he of desire to get involved in the celebrations but his constitution wouldn't permit it.

In D David BBEECKHHAAMM in D DAAVVIIDD BEECKHHAAMM MMyy SSoonn, Ted Beckham remembers a night when the couple were waiting for David returning late from a game. David went out to the night, and we were sleeping soundly at the time he arrived back home according to Ted. The next morning, we were awakened by a harrowing crash and banging sound as he ran to the bathroom. As soon as we awakened, he was suffering from a stomach infection in the bathroom. It was discovered that David was only drinking two or three drinks throughout the night. Tony Adams at this time was drunk with four pints Guinness in the space of an hour.

With the booze-drinkers becoming real sportsmen, the 1995/96 season was expected to be among the most exciting during the brief existence of the Premiership. The biggest opponents were Newcastle. Kevin Keegan had been appointed manager and was promoting an open, attacking style of football, much to the praise from the media and football fans. A remarkable run of wins in the early part of the season put Newcastle in the lead at the half-way time they had remained seven points better than United and had racked up 43 points after 18 matches

Two victories by 1-0 between these two teams saw United to reduce the gap - and with any help from Cantona returning after a suspension. The striker scored his first goal in his comeback match against Liverpool and also scored several important wins, including one in the game at St James's Park. In front of his face and still a game left, Ferguson succeeded in winding down his opponent in a famous remark in the press, suggesting that teams fought harder than Ferguson's team. It angered Keegan to the point that, when he stood in front of cameras following Newcastle were able to get an impressive win over Leeds the team, he looked just like a dog who had bones. While Fergie's men beat Nottingham Forest 5-0, with Beckham scoring twice in the air.

Keegan totally lost his way after which he blinked, before he went down... And then he coaching his team in handing the award to United. David won his first gold medal within his first year with the team and he was one game from winning number two. Manchester United were in the FA Cup Final against Liverpool and a particular prodigy was named Beckham was able to secure the winning goal in the semi-final against Chelsea.

Mai Manchester United 1-0 Liverpool FA Cup Final 1996

The FA Cup clash was the last nail to be put in the coffin for Liverpool's hopes that the next generation could be able to bring back the glory from the past decade. The talented and flimsy "Spice Boys'

As the golden boys Steve McManaman, Robbie Fowler, Jamie Redknapp and Jason McAteer were dubbed, they were deemed to be fake messiahs. Calamity the goalkeeper David James, was the stylist who ultimately was blamed for the gaudy cream Armani suits the Liverpool players wore upon their the day of their arrival at Wembley. The apparent disconnect between fashion and football was interpreted in the time as an expression of Liverpool's erroneous priorities. Nobody knew that the team with whom they were competing was a player that would be a symbol of both.

United's loose-haired tyro proved to be an all-round force and his first opportunity in the game went at his feet after just five minutes. He received a pass by Ryan Giggs and dispatched a stunning shot at goal which David James did well to keep out. James was, in all likelihood, Liverpool's top player.

Additionally, they have a great chance to save from Cantona as well as being active than Manchester United's Peter Schmeichel in a tight match.

In the midst of a heated and tense 90 minutes Beckham was able to take the left-hand corner which David James should have claimed. However, Dodgy Spice went back to typing and his inexplicably blunder at the ball was able to send it straight into the path the dangerous Eric Cantona.

While lingering over the D as he adjusted his body an incline backwards Cantona made the strike with a deadly power and accuracy across a crowded field of players. Liverpool fans watched with horror when the ball flew across the field and into the lower right part in the back of the net. It was now ended as Manchester United had achieved an incredible double. This was the dream debut year for David who was a consistent player player and it was almost a dream-like final in which he was a close second in the final to Roy Keane on a man of the match prize. As his place in the ManU's team secured and his mind was already focused on winning the chance to win an England award.

Man United Legend

David's talents were recognized by the newly appointed England manager Glenn Hoddle, who called David to play with Moldova on September. Hoddle was appointed to the England post over Terry Venables, who had led the team to the Euro 96 semi-finals, where they were unfortunate to defeat to penalties.

In spite of the defeat it was the return of England within the context of the world of football. There was a bit of surprise in Hoddle's selection, considering that Hoddle had not won any prizes during his period as a manager, it was because he was seen as an innovative thinker. Even though Venables had the advantage of being the best manager but there were constant issues regarding Tel's financial situation and he had no qualms in a drink. It was difficult to believe that Hoddle, for instance, Hoddle supporting group bonding sessions inside the "dentist's chair" in the Hong Kong bar.

The new manager was an at the forefront of his choices as well as being more willing to gamble with youngsters than previous England manager. Paul Scholes was fast-tracked even as he struggled to make it into the team at United. Also, Hoddle clearly saw in David his abilities that he'd used in his playing.

First of all, David was already confirmed as a free kick expert. David was also a confirmed free kick specialist.

The striker had thrown several powerful free kicks during his collection of seven

goals from last season's campaign, hitting the woodwork with a few of the times, too. It could not be imagined for

Anyone other than Ryan Giggs to be on the field at United,

But David was already proving that he could be at a higher degree.

He'd made the point of working the time to work

Practice his free kicks then had a terrifying

capability (for goalkeepers, anyway) for benting the ball

around a wall in a frenzied manner and with a stunning

accuracy. This, along with the way he crossed, gave David

A priceless item in the armor of Fergie.

Even though David was not able to match the speed or explosiveness of his running style that the winger Ryan Giggs had, he did his best to play to his strengths. In the event that he got the ball from the left wing but it wasn't his speed however, but the vision of his opponent and the accuracy of his passes. At times, when defenders approached and he would be able to move the ball in dangerous places and not even look up as well, with his ability to bend a ball over the defender in front of him He almost never needed the need to beat someone to pass the ball. Because of Giggs engaging in enjoyment on the other side, United were a handful for any player and his ability to see the ball was so great that teammates would often ask for confirmation if he intended to see the ball in that way!

17th August Wimbledon 1 - 3 Manchester United FA Premier League 1996/1997

A proof of how reliable the radar proved to be was in the first game of the season that followed, at a time which saw David becoming an Manchester United legend at the young Age of just 21. At the end of the match with Wimbledon, David spotted Wimbledon goalkeeper Neil Sullivan a few steps off his goal.

David was about ten yards in his own half, wide to the right side, but he allowed the ball to stand, pulled back an arm and hit with a lengthy, long swinging shot in the direction of. This was the type of punt with a chance to be successful that is usually

generated a great deal of laughter from opposing supporters, which was ironic

The crowd was cheering and waving after the ball was safely sunk into the hands of the keeper, or sailed across the stadium.

However, this is one instance when that simply didn't happen.

The moment the ball came out of Beckham's left foot, the entire team could tell that he was right on target and that the ball was moving through the air in a steady manner towards the goal. Sullivan did not appear to be stranded far away from his goal, however he began to backpedal with a furious speed - with no success. The ball smashed on the goal and left the Wimbledon fans stunned and the United supporters euphoric. At the goal, Alex Ferguson could be smiling as Eric Cantona sat close to him, shaking his head in awe.

It was an unforgettable and unforgettable moment. A shot that created a nation-wide controversy, that was bound to keep repeating in news bulletins. A teammate Jordi Cruyff recalled something similar to this in Spain However, besides Nayim's powerful lob of volley over Seaman during the 1995 Cup Winners' Cup Final, English supporters had not seen anything similar to. Pele attempted to score from the half-way line of the 70 World Cup when he saw the goalkeeper kneeling and praying - the legendary Brazilian who was kneeling down position and praying the legendary Brazilian at the age of a year Englishman was able to score it with the open field.

It's ironic that the boots of magic weren't at all his own They were custom-designed for a aspiring wonderboy with Rangers, Charlie Miller, and also a desperately Beckham took them on loan for the beginning in the new season. The difference was irrelevant. The strike would later get voted Goal of the Decade. Two years after, United fans ranked it as the best among Best, Law and Cantona.

It was the time that the David Beckham legend was born.

Manchester United looked invincible that season. Beckham making goals of the month contenders in his arsenal week after week. An explosion against Liverpool and a chip in Forest and a banana against Spurs All spectacular, generally from out of the box. in the match against Spurs The entire game was amazing, but mostly out of the box. Game undefeated streak which David completed with a shot to equalizer against Chelsea. This was winning their second league title for the second time in succession. The team also enjoyed their most successful year to date with the Champions League, including a 4-1 win over an extremely-rated Porto however they lost in the semifinals to eventual champions Borussia Dortmund. The season was one of the best for David who won the prize for most important goal of The Season, naturally and he also took home The Young Player Of The Award and finished second in the Senior player Of The

Year voting. He was the first player to win his first caps in England as well, he started his second season with the status of the Man United legend, never even a regular, and believed he would be able to get in the England team for the upcoming World Cup finals, having participated in every qualifying match. When it comes to football, nothing happens as it is supposed to. In fact 1997/98 could be his toughest season of his life but there was some comfort in between all of the failures.

Manchester United were looking like an irresistible force in football at the time that the season was beginning to kick off. The unexpected departure of Eric Cantona seemed to be a momentary sign that it could make the team unstable however, Ferguson was the most important player for the club at present. When his previous gamble ended well, he had the complete confidence of both the supporters as well as the board. They were such a deep team with so many capabilities that it appeared they were able to absorb the loss of their captain of the club. Incredibly inspirational Roy Keane was probably even more qualified to fill the position as he demonstrated. To take over Cantona's spot, Ferguson bought veteran Teddy Sheringham from Spurs. One year after his success in Euro 96, he seemed to be a perfect short-term replacement for the principal striker.

In September, the situation changed dramatically as Roy Keane was badly injured after a fight with Alf-Inge Haland. The Reds were without a captain throughout the season. The Reds were favourites to win the trophy once again however a trip at Highbury in November sent alarm bells.

Arsenal was now run by Arsene Wenger, a lucid French trainer who was swiftly becoming a guru.

they have become one of the best team in the nation. They scored two fantastic goals in the first half against United during the opening half hour by new players Anelka and Vieira as well. Despite the fact that Sheringham was able to drag United to a draw, following a ruthless second-half press David Platt fired Arsenal to the famous win. United came back from defeat and took an advantage, but they couldn't manage to overcome the Gunners even though they had two games left.

The trouble is that, as they say, don't come by themselves, but as a team In the end, Manchester United were beaten by Barnsley in the fourth round in the FA Cup. ManU was the club that which other clubs were hoping to defeat and with their absence Keane the team now stood greater chance of winning. Fergie required them to defend more and, even with the loss of their normal ability, it wasn't Arsenal. Even under Wenger "boring Arsenal was becoming less boring. But it wasn't just Arsenal that changed their look. The moment Liverpool released infant-faced Michael Owen in the 1-1 draw at Old Trafford, he'd made Gary Pallister look like he required an Zimmer frame in order to move through the game a little faster.

David is an established player in David was a regular in the England team. However, Glenn Hoddle was making heavy storms during qualifying to play in the 1998 World Cup. In the latter part of 1997, England played Italy at Wembley in one of the most crucial matches of their qualification group. Glenn Hoddle was given a instruction on how to win international games by Cesare Maldini's team. They was able to block England's attack as they hacked and probed for the ultimate move. As it arrived, David was able to only watch from the far distance. The goal opened the way for the sole goal of Gianfranco Zola. England had to be worried.

The final result was that the only chance for England to get to the Finals consisted of getting to Rome and preventing Italy from winning. The result was a draw 0-0 nevertheless, but one that was thrilling nonetheless. witnessed Hoddle beginning to understand familiar with international matches. Hoddle was able to mastermind a defensive system and occasionally a lightning attack on the goal. He basically beat Italy in their own way With everyone from Ian Wright and Paul Gascoigne playing.

Becks performed admirably throughout both matches and showed more and more confidence in free kicks and corners that were consistently testing defences. He looked like a footballer who was picked to play for England. Maybe not the most prominent name on the sheet of your team, however, you can leave it due to injuries. He was the sole England player who played in every one of the eight qualifying matches.

David displays his England shirt. Unfortunately United's grip over the Premiership started to slip away in the middle of the home stretch, they dropped their winning ways and in the meantime, Arsenal's Arsenal had come to the fore. They went to Old Trafford in March and Marc Overmars wreaked havoc on the left side as their defense remained sturdy as a stone. David as well as Gary Neville were on high alert throughout the day with regards to Marc Overmars' sporadic visits and it came as no surprise that he clinched Arsenal's win with a superb strike.

All of this was a part the final game of the season for Arsenal when they recorded an incredible unbeaten run which had teams hurled into the ground with scoring from their games ahead eroding United's advantage. After that, in the Champions League, United were defeated by a shrewd Monaco team who proved to United that they have much to be learning when they were slammed out of the quarterfinals. This was the very first time in the history of United in which David did not win trophies however, not all awards come from the game.

In the spring of 1997 David was involved in a pivotal meeting with a person who seemed to be far from football. Following a match for charity and meeting with Victoria Adams, also known as Posh Spice of The Spice Girls. It was revealed that the Spice Girls were actually just created by pop icon Simond Fuller who also created

PPoopp IIdollss and saw the market was there for a girl-only group that were raunchy, flirty and embodying"Girl Power'. Fuller provided them with funny names, and commissioned songs made of bubble gum and then pushed the group into a cult following. The year 1977 was the time when girls Ginger, Scary, Baby, Sporty and Posh were all over the place: they were the most well-known people across the nation and extremely wealthy. At the time that David came across Victoria in 1977, they were close to getting a movie released. He was the first to inquire about an autograph.

David's preferred genre of song is rap. He'd previously expressed desire to visit Victoria following an Spice Girls video. He had told Gary Neville, 'I like this one, with the short skirt and the hairstyle. I'm going to have to see her. Prior to that his football style had been a part of customs by sticking to blonde models, but Posh and her chic hand-free looks and cool style attracted David's attention. David later said that he was a fan of gentle girls and blondes however, Victoria is completely different with her dark and loud appearance.'

There was never any acclaim or fame for his chat lines. He when he was introduced to his girlfriend, he she said "I really like the necklace. It's really beautiful on you. The woman didn't recognize his name, but, recognizing that the fact that he wasn't sophisticated and likely impressed, pointed at it and declared, 'Million and a half pounds.'

He looked at him and then asked"How much?" She almost rolled her eyes at his incredulity. This was really just an ornament for a costume and she was convinced he'd be clever enough to call to use his cell phone. After he presented it to her, she rang it into her mobile. "Now, you've got mine," her voice told him.

Then he said to Gary "I didn't look at the necklace. I was just looking at her Tits.' David was already recognized as a shagger, and was a race sure thing to call her.

Much like many names, Posh didn't bear much connection to the background of Victoria. Her father was an electrician from London. London electrician, who got married to an East End girl called Jackie who was determined to get away from her humble beginnings. Her mother instilled Tony with a desire to succeed and the two established an electrical wholesaler, which was extremely lucrative. They then moved into a luxurious mansion in Goff's oak, Hertfordshire, complete with a kidney-shaped pool, as well as electronic gates. Tony was also the owner of the luxury of a Rolls Royce, which he took Victoria to school nearby in Chestnut and it was that touch of luxurious that lead her to be referred to by her peers for being "Posh".

Victoria spoke to a journalist about their first interaction"I realized the moment I saw David that among the things that was attractive about David was the fact that he had the same kind of family values and beliefs as I did. I loved the fact that he was a family man.' Victoria was already well-versed in PR and had been a regular participant in deceiving the media. She knew immediately the fact that David was an adolescent boy, and the very first lesson she was required to impart to David was that the time as the typical lad's girl was long over. Since she was two years older than David smarter, more wealthy as well as more savvy, it was not hard to get her convince David that if he went out with her, he could do it with the understanding that he wouldn't be sleeping around.

In the beginning, no one but Britain's famous paparazzi spotted this piece of HHeelllo the heaven. Victoria was much more well-known than David during this period as well. The Spice Girls were still going in the right direction, therefore there was no need for Victoria to make the relationship public. But, it was unnoticed because they remained discrete. The majority of the time due to his obligations in the field of training and the tours she was on and travels, they were only able to stay connected via phone.

David was already working on an application for his mobile. He's an excellent texter and today there are three phones he uses that he uses for his family members, another for his football team and one for his company management - and is racking up huge costs on each of the phones. At the beginning of the relationship between him and Posh his mobile phone was the only vital connecting point.

Chapter 12: World Cup 1998

It was evident that Fergie's concern or anger. Fergie is known for his dislike of the way mobile phones disrupt the training. A pre-game discussion with the team David's cell phone rang. He responded only to watch Fergie stroll across, take the phone from his hands and then, using a few appropriate expletives, throw it in the trash bin. Fergie was an earlier shop steward in the Clyde shipyards. His flamboyant behavior and his manner of speaking have never changed. Fergie is the Gaffer and nobody who is well-known or rich, could accept that without getting removed or being moved.

Footballers, of course, have been raised in a setting that can be compared to training camps, but with the huge difference that every professional player enjoys playing and recognize the discipline and control over their lives, which the management exercises. This is part of the game. For starters, Victoria Adams is not like many wives of footballers. When she first met David she was intelligent rich, opinionated, and made a name for herself in the business. Her reputation was bound to cause problems for a traditional disciplinarian like Alex Ferguson.

They didn't reveal their wedding plans up until the beginning of January 1998, which was nearly one year after meeting. In her presentation of the engagement ring worth PS140,000 before the press and said: 'I've seen the man who I believe that I'm likely to get older and wrinkled with. Also, it was World Cup year, so it was a time when tabloids faced an unprecedented media sensation and one of the nation's World Cup heroes was marrying one of the Spice Girls. The story could be made up however, when it became significant, why not.

Since then the two were referred to by the name of Posh 'n' Becks (it's not been that way before, but opposite) since their slang names were able to build an image of a brand that within a very short time, would become known around the world. When they were preparing for the World Cup, David was asked as often about his proposed bride as he was his participation in the World Cup. While Spice Girls were in the midst of a crisis. Spice Girls were facing issues because Geri Halliwell was deciding to step down from the group and follow a solo path, yet the interest of media was not overly high.

The somewhat aloof and batty Glenn Hoddle had an entirely different style of management than Fergie however in one aspect they had a lot in common in that they both didn't enjoy being part of the Posh 'n' Becks circus. The team was named by Hoddle for a trip to France to start their practice for their tournaments, warm-up games and bonding exercises. David was the most important member of the team.

The England's World Cup of 1998 will be known as one of the biggest tabloid events of all time. When the team assembled in France and put to the test, Glenn Hoddle was eyeing two persons in particular and questioning their abilities to tackle the challenges to come. The shocker came when he was forced to list those who were not included in the team which would reduce the number of players down to just 22.

When Paul Gascoigne had been almost similar to his previous self

England faced Italy in the qualification matches. it was starkly evident

Some, like Hoddle one, Hoddle be a part of some, including Hoddle, that he couldn't play in a World Cup again. Drinking (often in a sly way) but finding it hard to stay focused

Games and questions hovering over him

regarding his fitness and weight, Hoddle had probably

He was too generous in taking his word as far as he has. in a dramatic

battle at the camp held in France, Hoddle had to

Tell the legend Gazza to inform him that he was to be taken away

returning to England together with five other people and watched the

Former England legends exploded right in front of his own eyes.

spiraling into incoherent chaos that is topped by

Smashing the in his hotel room.

Actually, it was an logical and hard-headed choice

to remove Gazza the axe, but a few tabloids were more blasé

With one person urging his immediate reinstatement

as well as launching vicious tirades at Hoddle. Hoddle is the most hated of them all.

the team backed Hoddle's verdict, but it is it appears that Hoddle's decision is now in the hands of the

The honeymoon of the players as well as the manager ended.

It was evident that the two didn't have a lot of agreement on anything else.Gazza

Hoddle is remembered by some as one of the more challenging characters who have been brought in to control England

Hoddle: it wasn't so long that he'd been playing for himself and there was an impression that he believed that he was better than the individuals he was teaching. It was also in the field of training that Hoddle could be the most offensive.

In one instance, the team was practicing free kicks and corners, and Hoddle sought out players who were able to give the flick-back shot the distance. The type of shot that is used develops immense power, however few possess the speed required to put it in the right spot. If David had the chance to shoot, he did a bit of a mess as well. Tony Adams remembers Hoddle saying with a smile: "Clearly, David hasn't got this talent.'

Ted Beckham went one further and claimed that Hoddle came up to David and told him that he believed you were a good player. In any case, David was left shocked as well as humiliated. Many athletes, even those who were senior disliked the notion of a player an excellent striker of and being treated such a manner. However, the worst was yet to come.

Hoddle did not respect his reputation, but much of his actions were not only unpredictable, but also unique. Then, he decided Steve McManaman, one of the most recognizable famous players in Euro '96, was clearly not going to take role in the tournament On one occasion Hoddle was shown having a play with a ballboy as he waited for an interminable time for a non-essential substitute to appear in a warm-up session.

Hoddle's most shocking incident was his squad selection to play Tunisia. David was put in the stands with the Tottenham's Darren Anderton playing in the right-wing spot. When he saw the team's lineup, David asked to see Hoddle and Hoddle replied 'Not right now at my time, but later as he informed the media that David wasn't focussing enough in his soccer and was in fact the coded reference all of the players got towards be part of the Posh 'n' Becks circus.

Hoddle shouts at an England match

David was not pleased, but he remained true to his own opinion and let the tabloids to scream on his behalf into another outrage. There was even Alex Ferguson weighed in with his backing of David However, it was evident that Hoddle would not be affected only by the supernatural powers who he had consulted. Press reports were speaking openly to the group as the Hodd Squad. David was left to pray that he was brought in as a sub.

Hoddle's choice for his team was confirmed with a 2-0 win over the good Tunisia team. David appeared briefly but the praise was for his United teammate Paul Scholes, who scored the other goal with a stunning curving shot straight from the Becks text. However, this was going to be England's most straightforward game in group stages as a more difficult battle was before them against Romania.

June 22 England 1 and 2 Romania World Cup 1998

Romania had a great team and had a number of Premiership players who had a good understanding about the English manner - but England is still the most popular. Again, Becks was on the bench with Liverpool boy wonder Michael Owen, who was in the process of making an appearance at the finals. It was not the form book as Romania was on top form in the beginning in the second half and then scored the first goal through Coventry's Moldovan. At that point, Becks was in the game after being substituted for wounded Paul Ince.

In the second period without any sign of an opening goal, Hoddle became rattled and replaced Michael Owen for Sheringham. In a flash it was as if the England team was infused with fresh energy as Owen, Shearer and Beckham were able to connect. In the end, Owen hit at the 83rd minute following having been put in position through Alan Shearer and it looked like they'd be share the lead within their group with points against Romania but, after 90 minutes Chelsea's Graeme Le Saux was suckered by teammate Dan Petrescu, who scored with Seaman's feet. The result meant that England in need of a draw with Colombia in order to progress to the next round of 16.

Hoddle 1986

June 26 Colombia 2 - 0 England World Cup 1998

Hoddle was unable to afford the indulgence of his eccentricities. He inserted Owen and Beckham as his first choice players. Colombia are a skilled team that could outdo every team. The string-puller for Colombia could be Carlos Valderamma, the rangy midfielder, who wore what appeared like a rainbow of tumbleweeds on his head.

But, it was going the day for England: within 20 minutes Andererton scored the Owen cross over the upper corner of the Colombian net. Ten minutes later, Ince was sent off within of the Colombian 18,-yard line. Beckham used the free kick masterfully manner. Beckham stood on his left, and was looking at the wall, which the teammate Paul Scholes was trying to cause trouble. The Colombian goalkeeper was not sure what angle he should aim at and the leg-up offered him the impression that he didn't know. David played the ball through the hole which Scholes caused and to the left side of the net while the goalkeeper squeezing in the air. Hoddle ran up into the air with joy and David went over to the England crowd to scream. England had been eliminated... for the final battle against"the beasts" Argentina.

Every match between England and Argentina in the game of football is widely looked forward to and rarely let us down. A significant part of the legend is England's victory by 1-0 in 1966. Rattin was dismissed and Alf Ramsey made a pointed comment following the match, "The way some of the players behaved in the tournament reminds me of the behavior of animals.'

However, the game of 1986 when Maradona played the ball

Score and score perhaps the best World Cup

The most famous goal, one of the most famous. It took England out of the tournament.

of in the World Cup and, in certain Argentinian views, likely

to make up for made up for Falklands. This was the final meeting

There was a rift between both sides and England was determined to take revenge

the loss.

Adams' shot was saved by the Colombian goalie

June 30, Argentina 3 - 2 England AET [Argentina took 4-3 after penalties[Argentina won 4-3 on penalties World Cup 1998

The game in 1998 may have been the greatest: an incredible soccer match in which the teams played more evenly than at any time before. England played the first game using exactly the same 11 players who finished the match against Colombia. They took to the field in the most intense energy that has ever been witnessed at the World Cup - the compact stadium in St Etienne that was already known as the "pressure cooker" and this one was perfect to be it. In the first five minutes after start, England were a goal in the wrong direction following a penalty decision. Seaman was found guilty of having caused injury to Simeone within the penalty area. Batistuta took the penalty and England lost to the two time World Champions. The game ended in a tie after ten minutes after Owen fell in the Argentinean region. Shearer scored for England with the ball crashing into the left-hand area in the goal.

The next moment of the battle between Argentina and England. It is typical of the fantastic flowing football that took place that transpired on the night. David hit a beautiful ball to Owen who was left within a large free space. He then instinctively ran toward the goal of Argentina. He was swarmed by Chamot who was awestruck by the acceleration that the Liverpool striker, and then was followed by Chamot. Owen continued to push toward Ayala and then, in a stunning move the forward sped past him in a rush to swoop the ball the right side of his foot when Paul Scholes was screaming for the ball to go in the more favorable place. This was an iconic, fast finish, which was a testament to his years.

The goal was a masterpiece with one of the top defenses around even though he was just 18. David is the very first player to hold Owen and express his gratitude to him yet again, the Beckham-Owen team was considered as crucial to the England team.

A minute later, Paul Ince nearly put England more ahead But his 35-yard strike crossed the goal line but fell over the crossbar. In the final second of the half left, Campbell fouled Lopez just in front of the box. This free kick resulted in the perfect example of soccer brilliant. Veron was the one to take the ball and crossed the ball over Zanetti who ran behind the England wall. He appeared to be ghostly near the penalty area, shooting into the goal by using his less powerful left foot. Thus, both teams walked into the half-time ceremony honours in a thunderous applause by the fans.

The team did not make any changes either side prior to the start of the second quarter however, within a minute after that, the match was tilted in Argentina's favor in a wild sequence of events which has become the norm of World Cup previews on TV. David played his usual fierce game on the middle of the field. Even though David was put to guard against the less subtle strategies that were employed by Argentineans however, he was sparked by a brutal challenge to the Inter player Diego Simeone. Simeone not only knocked David to the ground, but also got his hair pulled back and slap him, in the midst of a scene where an England player was observing the grass rise at the player.

It was almost acceptable manner to David to shoot an uninhibited leg at the Argentinean however Simeone wasn't done and fell to the ground, providing a stunning appearance of the Spanish Civil War soldier being photographed in Robert Capa's legendary work of photojournalism.

The unfortunate thing is that this incident took place before the Dutch referee Kim

Milton Nielsen, who is not known to miss an opportunity to dismiss the player off. The referee waved his red card to David and threw the card back into his pocket within a snap and, despite the fact that there were some players playing on the pitch with familiar with the practice of yelling at referees but no one particularly David was in much of a hurry to contest the decision to dismiss.

The whole thing happened so fast that it appeared as it was David was standing up and left the field: Victoria was glued to the TV in America and was crying in her eyes. Meanwhile, his parents were sitting in the stands, still uncertain the reason for his being dismissed or not. A grumpy Hoddle did not pay attention to him as Becks passed him before heading down the tunnel towards changing rooms.

David was watching TV alongside the majority of Britain watching as England players played a rearguard performance that was just as thrilling as the Alamo There was one frightening moment in which the Argentines appeared to have an extra penalty. Then England scored on an angle, which Neilsen quickly disallowed as a few England players were celebrating, Argentina were able to break away and almost scored. It was an thrilling games that every person that watched it will remember and, given a half chance, will talk about till the cows go back.

However, nobody laughed and none of them was David who was in the stands when the additional time was coming to an end, and penalties followed. England have been criticized as being abysmal when it came to penalties and took the same approach. When Alan Shearer and Owen scored outstanding penalty kicks, Paul Ince and David Batty took a slack of their penalties... Argentina were eliminated. In a flash, the inquiry was not focused on the excellence of the England performances or even a couple of poor penalties, but Becks the act of treason.

Ian Wright summed up the conclusion:

Without being harsh to David Beckham, he cost us the game.'

As the players left on the pitch, David apologized to everyone in a resounding apology. Tony Adams, David revealed that he was particularly favorable to him. 'He was amazing for me,' David declared. When asked about Hoddle's response, he stated:

"He did not speak to me.'

It was further aggravated due to his parents' presence outside the arena. His father's expression at him brought to mind the magnitude the childish gesture of pity: "That was the lowest point of my life as the whole thing shook me. . . I've never had the tears I used to do when I was a young child. It was a long time I lost it.'

As this took place, Glenn Hoddle was keen to make sure that the media did not make Beckham not the blame for England's premature exile from the tournament and said: "If we'd stuck eleven against 11 then we may have performed something.' Beckham felt he was being treated as being a thief and wasn't in the slightest bit wrong. The Mirror featured the headline as 'Ten Brave Lions and One Stupid Boy' - the paradox was that the paper was clamoring for the boy's participation in the team only several weeks before.

However, it was even worse for his parents as they were a snooty target for culprits. David and Victoria frequently traveled and frequently within exclusive circles while his parents, who were ill-treated, trapped in a working class white province called Ingerland. The couple received so many threatening calls from the phone that they contemplated switching the number but decided against it due to the fact that Ted employed the number to run his own business.

While the non-Manchester United supporters prepared for a plethora of vulgar songs and shouts of Victoria and their sexual life. It appeared that this would be the toughest season to date, but because He set out to prove that his critics were right, 1998/99 would become one of his finest.

Chapter 13: A Golden Year

The 1998-1999 seasons began as poorly as one could. Manchester United played Arsenal in the Charity Shield and were given the 3-0 blow: it was only an exercise, but it was a loss that caused a lot of pain to the club. Also, David was harmed to the point of being constantly slapped on the back every whenever he came near to the ball. The next day, nearly every photo in the magazine's back page contained a multitude of Arsenal fans behind him making outrageous gestures.

It was the time to dig into. The day that kicked off the campaign seemed like a an excellent one, and the striker scored one of his signature free kicks in a draw match against Leicester. With effigies of him being hung on the gallows the game was likely to be an extended rehab. The man began gaining favor with media, and launched the charm offensive by publishing pieces like that published in the London-based list magazine TTiimmee OOuutt, which showed the man in a Jesus-like posture and dressed in all white The 'resurrection' David Beckham was the caption.

However, it was with football where he came back to himself, first alongside teammates from his Manchester United team-mates and then with fans. He arrived for practice in the preseason and was surprised to see all the players performing his famous kick to Simeone and that kind of joke was what he required to boost his mood. "I thoroughly enjoyed it, the coach said. 'As when I entered the room all of the players began falling to the ground and flapping their legs. I sat there, and smiled.'

When he and his team began a three-pronged campaign for the year that included the Premiership and the FA Cup and the Champions League The fans reacted to the renewed determination of the team as well as Becks. In the national arena the team was Arsenal yet again, and with an exciting new striker Nicolas Anelka, who were their main adversaries and match between them was becoming ever more heated. The last time they played at Highbury United, they were defeated by a score of 3-0, however after Roy Keane storming back into the team, there was an increased vigor towards United that the supporters appreciated. The fans were able to see that even with this loss United are determined to make amends for not having winning a trophy. However, no one spoke of the triple. But, at least not until now.

In the second game, which both teams had during the new year It was a tense game that saw Roy Keane and Patrick Vieira nearly going out and playing like men. In the second half, Arsenal were in control. United were able to fight back with a Andy Cole header from a Phil Neville cross on 60 minutes was the result that left both sides with honours. The team of Cole as well as Dwight Yorke with Becks as the primary provider seemed to represent the forefront in the development of United. As an assister, Becks's goal scoring tally from free play was affected, however Becks was never an admirer of the game and was relegated with the current system.

The FA Cup Fourth Round, the team's determination was evident in the match against rivals from the past, Liverpool. Scholes and his team had experienced little luck in the past at Old Trafford in the 90s However, this time the first goal scored by Owen showed that the game changed. In spite of the fact that the game the game was clearly favoring United, with Keane and Scholes as well as Keane not having luck. As the game progressed, it seemed like a 1-0 win for Liverpool. In the 85th minute an Beckham free kick provided Dwight Yorke a close-range equaliser two minutes later, Solskjaer, a substitute, landed the ball at the edge of the area and hit into the goalkeeper. Liverpool suffered a sigh of relief, with a couple supporters who were crying stunned.

United then followed that by hammering 8-1 Nottingham Forest (still a Premiership record) and their record in the face of the formidable Champions League sides had all of Europe discussing. United had two memorable matches against Barcelona at home, with both away, which ended with a score of 3-3. In the first game at Old Trafford, Beckham scored with a stunning free kick. Barcelona had to depend to Luis Enrique and Rivaldo penalties for a draw. At the end of the game, in Camp Nou there was a spectacular display of all-out offensive football from each team, something like that is rare within the current game.

Barcelona had the lead within minutes, but United scored a goal through Dwight Yorke. Andy Cole made it 2-1 shortly after the half-time break. Barcelona really needed to victory or else they'd be just about out of contest, but they battled back to draw 2-3 after the Rivaldo free strike. After that, United came back into the lead with the help of a Yorke goal but only to allow Barca to level the score again, making it 3-3. Yorke and Cole had a blast the night before, playing superbly. However, David was equally impressive in passing and crossing as an experienced player. The outcome effectively drove Barcelona from Europe however, United continued to be on track for a return trip in the Nou Camp for the Final at the end of that season. The team faced another European big name in the quarterfinals of the tournament: Inter Milan, complete with a player who was already well-known to Becks. The clash between David as well as Diego Simeone just 9 months ago since the great 1999 World Cup game was always bound to be make a lasting impression. What did David react? And, more importantly, can United demonstrate that they are worthy of a place against the imposing Italians? That was the answer. Beckham did a fantastic job with ability and poise, resulting in two goals that were scored by a spectacular Dwight Yorke. United beat the Italians away in a stunning opening half of attacking, passing football.

The second half was a different story. Peter Schmeichel pulled off a number of spectacular saves, including at one point to stop Ivan Zamorano, while Henning

Berg smashed the ball over the line. United had the utmost determination not to concede Inter this crucial goal away. And to top it off, Simeone had a goal not allowed for pushing. Beckham got his revenge, and United had a great set-up to play a rematch at the San Siro where Inter were kept at bay. United had the chance to play an equally great Italian side: Juventus.

However, prior to that they were in another semi-final at The FA Cup against Arsenal. It was the final season in which FA Cup semi-finals went into replays. This due to the fact that their fixtures were getting clogged up, was probably the last thing United had to worry about. The Premiership Arsenal were chasing United to the end It was looking that this game could be going through the wire. Three matches were played during the Champions League, of course. Then, what about what about the FA Cup? They had to defeat Arsenal. The game was governed by Sod's Law. even though a player was red-carded, Arsenal forced a replay. Jaap Stam claimed that after the three-point win was secured that Arsenal had more problems than other teams all time. It was now time for a rematch between Arsenal and Chelsea just days prior to the semi-final's second match against Juventus.

April 14th Arsenal 1 - 2 Manchester United (aet) FA Cup Semi-Final 1999 (Villa Park)

The most recent FA Cup semi-final replay was filled with excitement from beginning until the end. The two giants of English football battled for 120 minutes, and the match was everything. In contrast to the hacking contest, it was a an epic football feast. The game exploded into action with Becks made his mark in the seventeenth minute. The one thing missing from that season for David's game was his stunning shots from anyplace within and around the penalty box and it was a good thing for United the team, he opted for the game to compensate the time lost. When he was set up with Teddy Sheringham' lay-off, David glanced at the ball once before launching a stunning 22-yarder in the Seaman's top corner.

After holding Arsenal out for 69 minutes, the Dutchman began a looping race just 25 yards from the goal. The shot was directed towards the goal, and the ball was snatched away from Stam and was swung towards the back into the back of the net.

The game then took on quite a twist when Arsenal was celebrating a "winner" of Anelka when he took advantage of Schmeichel failing to take a shot by Bergkamp, only for referee David Elleray to uphold the high flag of the linesman.

Chapter 14: Mclaren Confronts Ellery

Then Arsenal was awarded an injury-time penalty. Phil Neville brought down Ray Parlour in the middle of the pitch as he blasted through the goal: it was just two minutes before the end of injury time. Bergkamp shot it with precision just in front of the upright however Schmeichel was quick, read the ball accurately, and then made one of those eye-reading saves which give penalty shooters the heebie jeebies.

Irwin takes on Parlour ManU v Arsenal FA Cup Semi-Final 1999

So again, for the second time in the space of four days, the teams were forced to play extra time and Arsenal continued to push forward in more number. United were put under tension in the closing period following the sending of Keane to another yellow card after attacking Overmars. A strike for Arsenal could kill

United off by this point but the team displayed incredible resilience and never say die attitude prior to Ryan Giggs produced one of the most memorable FA Cup goals ever in the 109th minute, following the wrong pass of Patrick Vieira. As he walked up the field, the striker shifted across the field from left to right then right to left, then around and back again and left Vieira, Lee Dixon, Martin Keown, and, lastly, Tony Adams in his trail, with the ball was never able to leave his side all the way through.

The shot was stunning. from an angle of just seven yards wide of David Seaman, when it appeared like he might leave the pitch and run through. The shot was not long enough for Arsenal to react and suddenly, the Treble was in the hands of United.

Manchester United v Juventus Champions League SemiFinal 1999

Following a draw 1-1, United were the underdogs in the game, and the result was an encore of dramatic endings in a series of thrilling finals. The game could have gone better for United after they lost to two goals quickly The second goal came via an extremely unfortunate deflection off Jaap Stam. The team now required at minimum two goals to beat one of the most formidable teams in Europe at their home stadium.

There was no sign of improvement in the first half when Becks made a tackle at the end of the second half, and many of the United players looked stunned. In the midst of nothing, Roy Keane came charging through to hit the cross to the back of the net and they suddenly returning to the match. Then Dwight Yorke scored with a spectacular diving header, and the Stadio Del Alpi remained still. While United searched for an unlikely win, they received another blow after Roy Keane was booked and was subsequently ruled out of an participation in the Final. But he still drove his team to victory without a care as Andy Cole snaffled a chance at the end of the match and left the Turin team in shock. Then Becks and United were on the brink of two big finals, as well as a crucial Premiership match against Tottenham in the home stadium in the final day of the campaign. The season was coming to an euphoric conclusion.

May 16th Manchester United 2-1 Tottenham Premiership 1998/99

United were aware that they required an outcome to guarantee they could win their fifth League championship in the span of 7 years Premiership football, having begun with a lead of just one point of Arsenal. It was a tense and suffocating experience for United fans, who played on their radios and hoped that the results from Highbury as well as Old Trafford would go their direction. The fans were shocked at the moment Spurs were left with no other goal than honour to stake they had the "Theatre of Dreams' at the edge of becoming being a disaster as Ferdinand who was unable to find the net throughout the season long, slipped over the defence in the 24th minute, and swung an unintentional lob at the unlucky Peter Schmeichel.

The stranded Peter Schmeichel.

yard box. The striker smashed a bouncing, irresistible shot towards the goal which sailed through Tottenham goalkeeper Ian Walker like some laser-guided shot. After the break, Ferguson was replaced Teddy Sheringham with Andy Cole who had only been playing for two minutes when Ferguson snatched Gary Neville's ball that was floated by the player, taking two steps to master the ball and then clipped his ball into Walker. After a long time and a full time whistle, it was over with a roar that went through the crowd of 55,000. The tannoys sounded Queen's "We Are Champions'. United was playing at it again for the fifth time in 7 seasons.

22nd May Manchester United 2-0 Newcastle FA Cup Final 1999

The first 8 minutes of the match against Newcastle were more dramatic than any other Cup Finals. A blazing strike of the Newcastle's Peruvian Nolberto Solano, the booking of Newcastle's German midfielder Dietmar Hamman, an accident to Manchester United skipper Roy Keane and, in the process an early appearance of Teddy Sheringham off the bench. In 96 seconds, she scored a goal after a stunning one-two exchange and Andy Cole.

After that, Cole, who has had a habit of hammering on them against his former club, was pushed clear through a flurry of headers among Becks as well as Sheringham. The lob he lobbed into Steve Harper didn't have sufficient velocity to take the game towards the goal line together with Greek defensive player Nikos Dabizas, who cleared the goal to ensure that Newcastle on the field.

Becks was in the centre of midfield for this game along with

Solskjaer mostly on the right side and Sheringham on the to the front. and

It was yet again Sheringham she was creating havoc throughout the

Geordies' area. He was quick to recognize the ever-insane "He

Goals scored by Scholes who in the 53rd minute sluggishly made it to the finish.

United's second game of the day. The result was not for Toon. Toon

Army and when the whistle blew, Fergie and his team started

Another victory celebration. However, the most important prize lay in wait for their guests.

The 26th of May Manchester United 2-1 Bayern Munich Champions League Final 1999 [Nou Camp Barcelona]

Manchester United's European Cup final was played on the day that would have been Sir Matt Busby's birthday, and was scheduled to be Schmeichel's final game with Manchester United. The odds were not exactly rosy when the match began: United seemed to have put aside their poor form in the league for their most significant game they'd ever played. With the absence of Paul Scholes as well as Roy Keane, United were not recognizably; whereas Munich was in a dazzling form.

The Germans hit the ball after just five minutes of play, Becks appearing to be in a coma in the midst of a flurry of celebrations. Mario Basle struck a perfect free kick off the outside of the box that went into an opening within the wall, which was where Nicky Butt had been turned. Peter Schmeichel was completely wrong-footed. The game progressed and Munich's belief grew as the confusion of United struggling to keep up. Cole and Yorke had been getting into each other's way, rather than being in goalscoring positions. Becks shouted at them in anger in the opening half. The latter was playing in a new location in the middle the field and was not performing poorly either.

The majority of the second portion of the second United were huffing and puffing trying to score an equaliser against Bayern's skillful counter-attacking game and Lothar Matthaus in the middle of the field. After at 67 minutes Ferguson introduced a crucial change by bringing on Teddy Sheringham for Blomqvist. However, it was a one-way affair. Scholl struck his way over the United bar using a smart shot, but Jancker knocked the ball over the United post by kicking it off with an overhead strike.

As the time wore on, David was one of the United players who maintained their heads high. There was already an injury warning as he sped across the wing, and Gary Neville's strike caused a corner which David took advantage of to get. While he was doing so the player actually observed people putting the white and black ribbons from Bayern Munich on the trophy and then up in the VIPs. George Best was making an escape from the bar.

However, David was able to drive a cross towards the end of the box, where could have been a goal for Schmeichel had hoped to make a difference, but it ended up in Giggs who was unable to block it. the ball looked like it was heading wide. However, it ended up in the path of Teddy Sheringham who swung his right-foot to side-foot the ball into the goal from 6 inches. The Nou Camp was ablaze and the crowd eagerly awaited the extra time as well as the golden goal, and even heart-stopping penalties.

However, in the nick of time with barely a second to play, United won another corner. Becks kicked the ball towards the danger zone, where Sheringham could only manage to kick fifty percent of the ball in the box at six yards. The melee included Ole Gunnar Solskjaer - he'd just been in the area for for 10 minutes

He pushed the ball in the direction of the goal using a straight right foot for the most significant goal ever scored by Manchester United. Then Gary Neville said, 'It felt as if an event of a supernatural nature occurred.' Lothar Matthaus, who was exhausted at the end of the 79th minute and was confident that the victory was Bayern's the dugout, watching with utter shock, as if that he had been the victim of the intervention of God.

It could have been. The day was Matt Busby's 90th birthday If anyone could have deserved such a gift then it would be him.

Ole Solskjaer was mobbed by almost the whole team as well as players on the bench while Schmeichel made a cartwheel to his goal. The referee was forced to scoop several distraught Bayern players because they had to finish the last few minutes.

Just minutes before kick-off Bayern played a sloppy ball in the United box. Butt was cleared, and on time, 93 minutes 33 seconds the referee gave a full-time whistle which meant it was full-time and the European Cup came back to Old Trafford. The final was not, in all likelihood, the greatest football-related European Cup Final ever played however it was amazing.

The praises and accolades that came with this amazing British sporting accomplishment poured over the players, but Becks was given specific appreciation. Becks' fervent performances with United have erased the impressions of the 1998 World Cup in 1998 and it was as if he has come back from the dead to be one of the best well-known footballers in Britain.

In a personal sense as well, it could not have gone more perfect. The first child of his father, Brooklyn Beckham, was born in the city of Brooklyn, and was named after the location that he was first born. The moment he was born, Beckham stated that he had cried just like he had cried following the England match against Argentina but this time, full of happiness. The joy was heightened by his marriage to Victoria in the month of July, 1999 after his best season at Manchester United. Elton John even came in to entertain guests.

The wedding was held in Luttrellstown Castle near Dublin. Following a family-sized and close friend wedding ceremony (Gary Neville served as the happiest man) inside a private space in the castle, a large number of guests, attired in white and black upon request, enjoyed the slap-up feast, with champagne roses. Beckham was insistent

Chapter 15: Beckham Kisses Son Brooklyn

On his most loved dessert: sweet and sticky! What was the price? The two millionaires had already been sour about PS25 million, and a PS1 millon contract was signed by signing OK! for the exclusive rights to wedding pictures. Posh and Becks could make much more money from having a celebrity wedding than they did been singing and playing football.

Victoria was wearing a champagne-colored dress made of satin. It was created by Vera Wang. The ceremony ended when the couple released their doves of white into the sky and illuminated the sky with a an amazing fireworks display. The couple took off for a wedding in a luxurious house located on the Cote d'Azur.

There was one notable absence from the wedding. While he knew David when he was young Alex Ferguson had not considered going to the wedding, as he'd previously done along with Phil Neville. Ferguson was disillusioned by Becks"stardom-oriented lifestyle," and was not a fan of Victoria which that she reacted to with interest. Ferguson claimed he had always knew that this "fucking woman" had come going to Manchester due to the manner in which it affected him as a teammate. He was furious as well at the fact that Becks was able to go above and beyond to his club's chairman in order in order to obtain an additional two days of his honeymoon. Fergie decided to cancel it. Victoria declared his decision to be 'vicious and unforgiveable'. she did not forgive him or forget about it.

Following all the success as well as the glitzy, schmalz-filled wedding Becks and Fergie had a sudden collision path. It marked the start of the end of Beckham in Manchester United.

The England Captain of the England

With more options as ever before,

The 1999/2000 seasons was to be a mixed season for

Beckham has actually performed better in February over

halfway in the race for the title and he was further ahead than he'd been all the season. He was

an outpouring of media critique and attention to the lack of

assists and goals, it hit an all-time high just prior to when United played

Leeds during that time for an important Premiership game. The player was

The team was not in a class that resulted in an exploding disagreement in a heated argument with

Ferguson and then removed Ferguson from the team.

A constant source of tension was the career of Victoria in The Spice Girls, which he was constantly asked about just as like his own regardless of how many instances he said it wasn't something to do with the group. The group was fighting to recover from the disappearance of Geri Halliwell. A whole album was put on hold before it could be scheduled to release in November 2000. However, with Geri going, the group was left with no hope of a future.

Another source of distraction, although an enjoyable one is Brooklyn. Even with their extravagant lifestyles David as well as Victoria were committed parents. They were famous for never employing a nanny to all of their children. David is a parent who's hands on. He was shocked when the son was sick one Friday, he didn't attend school. Fergie whom was extremely hands-off with his dad could not believe what he saw. 'He dunno get run over. He was sick for Christsakes" was his reply. Yet, David stood his ground as Fergie confronted him about the fact that women's work was interfering with the training. Fergie became angry and removed David off the team roster for Saturday's match.

David was forced to stand glumly in the stands in the stands at Elland Road watching United win the title in the final game against Leeds. Fergie hit him in the areas it was most painful, keeping David from wearing the white shirt that which he was a fan from the time of his childhood. It was, however, an attempt to hit his bows from the Posh and Becks showboat that Fergie was accustomed to hating.

The rumours about a possible transfer started to circulate: Beckham was going to Arsenal, Barcelona, Inter... Arsenal were thought to be extremely attractive due to the fact that Victoria was not shy about revealing she was keen to be more in London and not Manchester. Victoria was also worried about the manner in which Fergie did not treat his players like the scouts he had. She felt it hindered David's capacity to capitalize on his image. This she knew would be, with the proper public relations machine, turn into a massive.

A person close to Fergie claimed that he has never been a fan of Beckham's wife Alex always stated that the he would never have David's lifestyle in Posh in the millions. He's protective of Beckham and is concerned about him as a victim of Posh's publicity machines and it does not fit his work as a professional.'

www.ingramcontent.com/pod-product-compliance
Lightning Source LLC
Chambersburg PA
CBHW071440080526
44587CB00014B/1933